"Fascinating and engrossing. Reading *Jujitsu Rabbi and the Godless Blonde* is like looking into the windows of compelling people you want to both meet and love. By the end of the book you will do just that."

—Jenny Lawson, #1 *New York Times* bestselling
author of *Let's Pretend This Never Happened*

"Rebecca Dana meets the jujitsu rabbi in the same place fairy tale meets reality, which is the same place all of us meet our lives: nowhere near where we expected. Let me be clear: I've never met the author, and I had neither the time nor the inclination to blurb this book, but I started reading her odd, engrossing, tragicomic coming-of-adulthood tale and couldn't stop."

—Deborah Copaken Kogan, author of
The Red Book and *Shutterbabe*

"I'm qvelling!! Rebecca Dana's brilliant memoir touchingly and daringly juxtaposes the mysterious world of Orthodox Jewry with the even more mysterious world of fashion. I was amused and verklempt, all at the same time."

—Simon Doonan, author of *Gay Men Don't Get Fat*

continued . . .

"Suffused with shimmering prose and a kick-ass spirit, *Jujitsu Rabbi and the Godless Blonde* is a brave and brilliant New York coming-of-age odyssey. With an eye for the damning detail and an ear for the heart-soaring quote, Rebecca Dana has delivered a devilishly funny true story brimming with pathos, oddball characters and beautiful revelations. I haven't enjoyed a memoir this much in years."

—Don Van Natta Jr, *New York Times* bestselling
author and Pulitzer Prize winner

"Rebecca Dana's story is a lot like New York City—bustling and busy, packed with Jews and jobs, faith and friendship, accident and ambition. With *Jujitsu Rabbi and the Godless Blonde*, Dana joins the ranks of women who have come to New York, forged identities on their own alongside improbable allies and lived to tell the tale with wit and grace."

—Rebecca Traister, author of *Big Girls Don't Cry*

"Rebecca Dana's funny, juicy memoir of her Brooklyn year with a most original housemate goes down like a terrific New York cocktail—with some sweetness, a snappy twist of sublime and plenty of heart."

—Julie Metz, *New York Times* bestselling author of *Perfection*

"This is the beautifully told story of every smart young woman's start in the big city, where dreams first come true and then they rain like hell all over you. Rebecca Dana is wise yet self-effacing, hysterical but dark. This book is the perfect photograph of the last agonies of being young."

—Choire Sicha, *The Awl*

"A fantastic read. Will make you want to take your life by the horns."   —Morgan Spurlock, filmmaker

"Dana is able to write hilariously about her temporary ignominy and the vicissitudes of her job as a fashion journalist because through it all she maintains an acute sensitivity for the absurd . . . And there are larger issues, such as which kinds of lives are worth pursuing, packed in along with the ground-level concerns of getting along with a crazy roommate."   —*The Daily Beast*

"A laugh-out-loud tour of heartbreak, fashion and the search for community in unexpected places."
                                  —*Pittsburgh Post-Gazette*

"[A] canny, buzz-inducing memoir . . . Funny, wily, audacious and captivating. Dana asserts her passion for glitz and high heels; vividly recounts her crazy adventures, profane and sacred; and saucily ponders life's big questions."   —*Booklist*

"Dana speaks, often hilariously, to the familiar tension between spiritual searching and an unabashed embrace of the superficial . . . Smart, tight prose and incisive humor."
                                  —*Kirkus Features*

BERKLEY BOOKS

Jujitsu Rabbi

and the

Godless

Blonde

A TRUE STORY

Rebecca Dana

THE BERKLEY PUBLISHING GROUP
Published by the Penguin Group
Penguin Group (USA) LLC
375 Hudson Street, New York, New York 10014, USA

USA • Canada • UK • Ireland • Australia • New Zealand • India • South Africa • China

penguin.com

A Penguin Random House Company

Berkley trade paperback edition ISBN: 978-0-425-26493-5

The Library of Congress has catalogued the
Amy Einhorn Books hardcover edition of this title as follows:

Dana, Rebecca.
Jujitsu rabbi and the godless blonde : a true story / Rebecca Dana.—First Edition.
pages cm
ISBN 978-0-399-15877-3
1. Dana, Rebecca—Friends and associates.   2. Journalists—United States—Biography.
I. Title.
PN4874.D315A3 2012
070'.92—dc23 2012029871

PUBLISHING HISTORY
Amy Einhorn Books hardcover edition / January 2013
Berkley trade paperback edition / January 2014

PRINTED IN THE UNITED STATES OF AMERICA

10   9   8   7   6   5   4   3   2   1

Cover art of fish by Shutterstock/Jag_cz; fishbowl by Shutterstock/Alex Staroseltsev;
statue by Gregor Schuster/Getty; NYC statue by Peter Zeray/Getty.
Interior text design by Meighan Cavanaugh.

Penguin is committed to publishing works of quality and integrity.
In that spirit, we are proud to offer this book to our readers;
however, the story, the experiences, and the words
are the author's alone.

To Nora

We tell ourselves stories in order to live.

—JOAN DIDION, *The White Album*

Contents

Jujitsu Rabbi

and the

Godless

Blonde

Prologue

It's ten o'clock on a Tuesday night, a light rain is falling on the wide streets of Brooklyn and I'm in my living room, strangling a rabbi.

This is the first time I've ever physically assaulted a man of God, and I have to say, it feels *excellent*. My fingers, with their chipped red nail polish, are digging into the soft white flesh of his rabbi neck. My heart is pounding loudly in my ears. Normally, I am the least violent person on the planet—a practitioner of yoga, a shopper for shoes—but in this moment, I'm completely unhinged. I'm a ballerina assassin, a ninja superstar, a platinum-haired dragon slayer in Stella McCartney vegan loungewear. Watch out, assholes: Jujitsu Blonde is *in the house*. (She lives here, actually. She was trying to read the December *Vogue* before turning in early on a work night, but then this bearded dude rolled up talking smack, and now she's on the path of destruction.)

Somewhere off in the distance, someone is blasting the 10,000 Maniacs on a wheezing desktop speaker system, and I can just barely hear Natalie Merchant whining about something, and I make a mental note to kick *her* ass someday too.

Who is this guy, anyway—this *Hasid*, this *pillar of his community*, this ginger-haired fucker with the squinty eyes and the placid demeanor and the beige yarmulke the size of a dinner plate bobby-pinned to his head? I want to smack the Coke-bottle glasses off his pale God-fearing face. Has he ever even seen the sun? I can tell he's wearing *tzitzit*, a religious garment, underneath his clothes because the fringe is hanging out like some short sham of a hula skirt. And the T-shirt he's got on over it is a trip: It has a drawing of Calvin and Hobbes on the front and a dialogue bubble with the words "New York Attitude." I'll show this gentle Yid some New York Attitude. I'll show him what two hours a day of Iyengar yoga and a bachelor's degree in American history and an encyclopedic knowledge of the last eight seasons of ready-to-wear from Paris, New York *and* Milan and a diet of sushi, soy milk and organic spinach—and, oh yeah, a broken motherfucking heart—can do. I'll send him back to Russia with a collapsed windpipe and no knees!

Because the night belongs to lovers!

You're next, bitch.

The rabbi twists around forty-five degrees and looks at me with one straining eye. We're basically the same size, only he has more padding around the middle, and he's wearing some heinous pair of frayed brown rabbi shoes that lift him up an extra half inch. But still I'm thinking: no problem. I don't care how "chosen" this flabster is, he's going *down*. My hands are steel claws. I tighten my grip, taking a moment to contemplate my options: Would it be better to body-slam him down right here in the living room or drag his limp carcass out into the courtyard first so everyone can watch? Then I notice the muscles in his back tense, and—*uh-oh*. There are muscles in his back.

In an instant, everything changes. He reaches up and grabs my wrists and performs some freaky Mortal Kombat maneuver, nearly stripping the delicately exfoliated and moisturized skin of my forearms from the bone. He pulls me toward him, into his damp right armpit, and holds me there for just one second, just long enough that I can see the fire in his eyes, just close enough that I can smell his breath: pizza. And then without warning I go down, I don't even know how, like one big bag of elbows clattering against the wood floor, blinkered and speechless, while above me, Cosmo the Rabbi grins madly.

Everyone has a fight-or-flight response, but in this case, both impulses strike me simultaneously. I want to run away, and I want to clock him. Fight *and* flight. Maybe it's a Jew thing. Observance-wise, Cosmo and I are opposites, but in the technical aspect, we are the same. Equal in the eyes of God and the SS, we are both genetically Jews, both members of a tribe that has been chased around the world, kicking and screaming—fighting while fleeing—for the last three thousand years. Millennia of genetic imprinting and a lifetime of poor impulse control nearly propel me in two directions, at him and away, but in the end both lose out, and I sit there, motionless, holding back tears.

"At this point I would stomp on your face," he says cheerfully. "Or kick you in the head, at least."

That's what happens when you fuck with God.

IN MY DEFENSE, he asked for it.

"Please, Rebecca," Cosmo had said. "Choke me!"

"No," I'd said. "Jesus! No."

I'd been curled up in my usual position on an emerald-green velvet armchair incongruously plopped in the center of our large, dirty, empty parlor. For nine days, the rabbi and I had lived together like this, in circumstances any sane person would describe as "sin." We were not involved, would never become involved—get that out of your head right now—but the means by which we had arrived at this point, and would remain suspended there, in awkward cohabitation for nine weird months, were, at a minimum, unusual. I am a twenty-seven-year-old nonpracticing Jew, a journalist who'd spent her adult life pursuing the feminine ideal as laid out by the *Sex and the City* television series. Cosmo is an ultra-Orthodox Lubavitch-Hasidic Jew, an ascetic, a practitioner of a faith that forbids an unmarried man and woman from being alone in a room together, let alone living side by side, separated by one thin wall. I don't know what the Talmud says about a rabbi drop-kicking a skinny girl in the middle of the apartment they share, platonically, but I suspect the scholars would frown on it.

There are a lot of complicated explanations for what was going on then in our shithole two-bedroom in Brooklyn—explanations that draw on ancient scripture and popular culture, that deal with the peculiar appeals and deceptions of modernity, the privilege of youth and the limits of faith—but for the time being, a simple explanation should suffice: I was broke. Rent was cheap. He needed the money.

A week before I moved in, Cosmo had taken up jujitsu. He was rapidly losing interest in God, so why not? He was not leading a congregation now. He was, instead, the smartest employee of the Fast Trak Copy Center in the neighborhood, where he duplicated keys and halfheartedly tried to rescue people's hard drives while dreaming of becoming a rock star. Whatever nerves the retail job hadn't destroyed, the creeping agnosticism had, and the godless rabbi needed an outlet. An amateur jazz historian with a six-year degree in philosophy, he spent much of his spare time playing the electric bass, for a time in a band called Denim Fajita, which he really thought was going somewhere, but which went nowhere. Fluent in six languages, he had briefly dated Leah, a Yiddish scholar who really got his motor running, until she ditched him. He had just wrapped up an extension course in introductory Portuguese, so, he figured, it made sense to study hand-to-hand combat next.

Jujitsu was great but also "gay," in Cosmo's estimation, since it involved rolling around on the ground with men. Whatever Maimonides might have thought of me, there's little doubt how he'd view that. Cosmo had just arrived home from jujitsu class when he began nagging me to choke him—he wanted to practice, and at least I wasn't a dude.

At last I obliged, taking a short break from wallowing, my activity of choice since moving in, days after a breakup that had sent the world as I knew it crashing down on my head. I was single, miserable and living in a muggy apartment in the middle of the Crown Heights section of Brooklyn, wherever that was. I figured I might as well fight a rabbi. That feeling changed abruptly when I found myself on the ground, nursing a bruised shoulder and two hinky wrists. He hadn't even really gone at me—it was all just pretend—but I hadn't eaten more than an occasional bowl of plain oatmeal since the breakup, and by that point, the pope could have done me in.

"*Ouch*, Cosmo," I say.

"Sorry!" he says, beaming, and trips off to make tea.

"You know, Rebecca, you should really do jujitsu," he calls from the kitchen.

In nine days, we had already been over this half a dozen times. Every time I fell into talking about my ex, every time I started to cry or wallow or reminisce about lost love, Cosmo would beg me to join him for a class. I had other outlets for my feelings, I explained. I was a writer. I worked out. I went to sample sales and cocktail parties and had long dinners with friends. I was a regular New York City gal, as I'd always imagined I would be: a Yale graduate, a social drinker, a reader of

Us Weekly and the *Wall Street Journal.* What I was not was the sort of person who got all sweaty rolling around in a leotard on a mat.

"Why do I have to do jujitsu, Cosmo?" I ask, for the seventh time.

He shouts over the screaming kettle, "Because it's just like sex, only without the sadness!"

He was morose, listless, hilarious—possibly a virgin, I wasn't sure. At a minimum, he should have been, if he'd really followed all the rules. Cosmo had come over from Moscow a decade earlier with a suitcase of clothes, a hundred dollars cash and a road map to Brooklyn—nothing else. He fancied himself a Raskolnikov, but his darkest vices were good beer and big boobs, which together had edged God largely out of his thoughts lately. He had a weakness for awkwardly translated Russian expressions of disbelief, the best of which was: "You could be from Mars for that price!" He played the bass, listened to psychedelic punk rock and watched *Top Chef* online, over and over, season after season, until he could recite the dialogue from the cable reality cooking show, on which contestants whipped up all kinds of delicious dishes that Cosmo, strictly kosher, would never be allowed to eat.

We had a surprising amount in common, for a Russian rabbi and an atheist from Pittsburgh. We were both only children, both broke, both alone and both well accustomed to fighting and running away. Cosmo's religion was Judaism, and it was failing him. My religion was a secular hash of things I picked up from books and movies during a boring childhood in the suburbs. I didn't think much about the next world, but I thought plenty about this one: the kind of person I wanted to be, the kind of clothes that person would wear, the man she'd date, the apartment she'd live in, the restaurants she'd go to and the items she'd order off the menu when she got there. I had done everything right, had followed all the rules for a happy adulthood, just as Cosmo had followed the strictures of Orthodox observance to the tiniest detail. Yet here we both were, lost and depressed. Our faiths had faltered. The stories we'd been telling ourselves suddenly stopped making sense.

I crawl up off the floor and back into the green velvet chair, while Cosmo carries in our tea. Mine arrives in a small brown cup. His is in a rainbow-striped mug the size of his head that says, in big letters, NO KVETCHING.

"What's gonna happen to us, Cosmo?"

"I don't know, dude," he replies, rolling a cigarette with loose tobacco from one of the dozen-odd Bali Shag bags lying around the apartment. "I guess we're pretty much fucked."

The Complete Story of
How I Got Everything
I Ever Wanted

One morning seven months after I graduated from college, I quit a job I never liked as a reporter for the *Washington Post*, jammed my wardrobe into a rolling suitcase and went to the train station without even bothering to look at the schedule first. It was January 27, 2005, a date I remember as well as my birthday. I arrived in New York in the middle of the afternoon, with twenty dollars and one credit card in my wallet and an expired driver's license that I didn't renew for three years. A week earlier, I'd secured a relatively firm but by no means ironclad commitment for a $24,000-a-year reporting job at the *New York Observer*, a small, salmon-colored weekly newspaper that I'd read for the first time two weeks before that. I owned no furniture and had arranged for no permanent place to stay. None of that mattered—I was home.

The taxi line outside Penn Station was long, so I walked a

block north, dragging my suitcase, with its one functioning wheel, through puddles behind me. Midtown seemed glorious in the winter drizzle. The fumes wafting out of sidewalk nut-vendor carts were warm and sweet. Steam puffed up around my ankles from the subway grates, and it looked a little like I was walking on clouds. It *felt* like I was walking over a fetid subway grate, but at that point I had trouble distinguishing between the look and the feel of things. Life looked right, and I was thrilled. Some girls imagine their wedding day when they're young: the dress they'll wear, the music that will play, the man they'll spend the rest of their life with. I imagined my first day in New York: the way it would smell, the first taxi ride I'd take, the people I'd meet in all the days thereafter and the life I'd live, down to the finest detail.

I am from Pittsburgh. Technically, I'm not even from the pea-size industrial city, glamorous as it seemed in my youth, but O'Hara Township, a small suburb to the north, non-descript in every way. I don't know who first introduced me to the idea of New York, but for as long as I can remember it has been my Jerusalem—the shining city off in the distance, the only place to go. I'd visited a few times before I moved there—exhausting, confusing weekend trips, once with my parents and a few times with friends—but by and large, my sense of the city came from books I read, TV shows I watched, mov-ies, pictures and stories in the newspaper.

I had read enough to know that New York was made up of three kinds of people: those born here (the Glass family, Ed Koch, certain hard-bitten tabloid news reporters); the commuters (my friend Matthew's father, a buyer at Macy's who specialized in women's intimate apparel and went home to Westport every night); and the people like Truman Capote, J. P. Morgan, Zelda Sayre and me, who came from somewhere else and gave the city its soul. In my mind, it was simply the place one went, as soon as she possibly could. What would I do there? I would work and eat and go to parties and watch TV on boring afternoons and fall in love, and eventually I would die—happy.

I looked north, up Sixth Avenue to the midtown canyon and Rockefeller Center and after that Central Park, and felt everyone else's stories falling like fresh soot from the skyscrapers above: Anne Welles and Neely O'Hara in their first apartment uptown. Faye Dunaway, braless under a chiffon blouse, smiling her taut smile on the executive floor of Union Broadcasting System. Holly Golightly stroking her cat on an idle Sunday afternoon. Diane Keaton shopping for Christmas presents on Fifth Avenue in a gentle snow, driving her beat-up Beetle wildly up the West Side Highway, staking out a town house with Alan Alda. And of course Carrie Bradshaw, clomping all over the place in her towering heels. To live in New York was to participate in the world's largest choose-your-own-adventure story, one that featured millions of possible adventures, all of which had already been chosen. I knew instinctively, from the moment I arrived, that my eventual obituary, should I merit one, could be plagiarized entirely from ones that had already been written. For a long time, this was a comfort to me.

In this way, everything about New York felt new and

daunting and wondrous, but at the same time, that wonder was weighed down by a layered foreknowledge of the New York experience—by the pictures and stories of everyone I was imitating, who'd already done every imaginable variation of this very thing before. As I took deep breaths of the damp, polluted January air, I already knew that there is no one in the world younger than a girl in a new dress on her first day in New York. I was authentically wide-eyed, but never quite *fully*, since I knew enough to recognize "wide-eyed" as a phase. What I didn't know then was that a life made up of fragments of other people's lives is still something materially new. A kiss on the Brooklyn Bridge is not every kiss; a reporting job is not every reporting job; a photocopy is not exactly the original. To understand this, you don't have to abandon your entire life, everything you ever wished for, and move in with a Xerox shop rabbi in Brooklyn, but in my case, it certainly helped.

When I left Penn Station that first day, I had never held a hand out into traffic personally. But I'd watched and read the stories of hundreds of others who had tentatively done the same, who had felt uncomfortable at first, had affected non-chalance and then gradually grown accustomed, so that even-tually the entire action of hailing a cab could be performed without any mental engagement, while on a cell phone and doing seven other seemingly vital things. When the taxi pulled up, I strained to come across as cool, even a little bored by the interaction. It was essential that the driver believe I was the sort of person for whom hailing a cab was no big deal. I climbed into the backseat, holding my damp suitcase in my lap and watching with horror as the meter ticked up. My first crosstown ride was an absurd extravagance, one I wouldn't truly be able to afford for years. But I did it anyway. The important thing was to ride across town. I could easily have walked, but the girl I wanted to be didn't walk with her luggage, and so the girl I was didn't either, even though it would have made infinitely more sense.

The cab took me to my first home in Manhattan, which was inside New York University's private hospital. Annie, my best friend, was a medical student there, and when I got to town I shared her concrete-block dorm room on the twelfth floor, directly above Emergency Intake. She had a foldout twin daybed and a wicker basket full of energy bars, to which I was welcome. Her narrow window looked out onto the East River and down over a giant white party tent left over from the autumn of 2001, when it was set up to house the charred remains of bodies recovered at the World Trade Center site. When I arrived, more than three years after September 11, it still held nearly fourteen thousand partial remains in three large storage cases, destined someday for a museum dedicated to the massacre.

Across the street was the 30th Street Men's Shelter, housed in the old Bellevue Hospital building, a large dark brick mansion with bars on the windows and an architectural style that conjures an abandoned leper colony. We could see some of the patients' rooms from her bedroom window, and they could see us. Occasionally, they backed up to their safety-locked windows and pulled down their pants. On my first night in the city, when I was walking back late from my first New York party, someone on one of the higher floors threw a dinner roll at my head.

At the time, Annie was doing a rotation in the psychiatry ward at Bellevue Hospital, a few blocks away. One of the patients in Annie's care was a classic schizophrenic. His particular eccentricity was that he thought he was a superhero. He was usually a benign presence in the ward, except for a few times a day. At these times, which came with clockwork precision, Annie would be in with other patients and would hear a few quick footfalls, followed by a loud thud—the sound of the schizophrenic trying to run through his bedroom wall. Against all evidence to the contrary, he believed this was his superpower. Annie would rush upstairs. The nurses would tend to his cuts and bruises. Someone would try to explain basic physics and the limits of human endeavor to the man. Then, a little later, he'd do it again. This struck me then as horribly sad, and it strikes me now as exactly what I've been doing my entire adult life.

After a few weeks, I moved out of the hospital and into a college friend's loft space in Brooklyn, where I lived for six months while he was away in an ashram. From there I went to a dilapidated brownstone nearby, which I shared with three twenty-three-year-old boys. Our landlord was a hairless, lobotomized widow who wore a bright red wig askew and went by the name Dr. June. Dr. June, who was not a doctor, lived on the first floor, which smelled like ointment. The three boys lived on the second floor, which smelled like socks and beer.

I lived on the third, which smelled like old wood and dust, with traces of socks and beer.

Neil, Burt and Max were bighearted Ivy Leaguers who divided their time between getting stoned on our couch and picking up chicks at Pianos, a bar on the Lower East Side. They were all devoted students of New York's mating rituals, and together, they'd developed a signature move: Just before last call at Pianos, they would start talking rapturously about the next morning's brunch. Banana pancakes. Mimosas. Big, fluffy, buttery, cheesy omelets and orange juice to go with them and crispy, salty home-fried potatoes and maybe an order of Belgian waffles with vanilla ice cream on the side. Women found this irresistible. I know, because I found many of these women in my bathroom the next morning, getting ready for brunch. Neil, Burt and Max called me "Jane" for Jane Goodall, who lived with the apes she studied.

My experience with men had been limited up until that point. The first love of my life was Dirk Skellershmidt, a gay eleven-year-old who shared my cockpit at Space Camp. I was the commander of our fake mission into orbit, and he was some low-level peon who climbed around outside and pretended to hammer things. He used to come visit me and perform song and dance numbers from theater camp while I prepared for graver tasks, like fake reentry into the earth's atmosphere. "I think you love Dirk," said Justin, another Space Camper, who wore a different baseball-themed Jesus T-shirt every day.

"Why?" I asked, and in response Justin pointed to my own

T-shirt, which was from Hidden Valley Ski Camp. I looked down and saw a blob of chocolate icing marring the "id" in Hidden Valley, possibly the entire "idden."

"You were staring at him all through lunch," he said. Apparently so intently that for the first time in my entire young life, I took my eyes off of *cake*.

Yes, I had to agree, this was probably love.

The second love of my life was Johnny Depp, and also the third, a love that faded and then burned with renewed intensity whenever he came out with a new film. The fourth was Doogie Howser, child-prodigy doctor of prime-time television, and the fifth was my friend Libby's dad, who was tall and appealingly WASPy. These mild attractions all developed and disappeared—unrequited, of course—before I turned twelve. I was a late bloomer and did not date much in high school, as you might expect from a girl who spent her childhood at Space Camp, rolling around in chocolate cake. By the time I got to New York, I had had two odd, unsatisfying, semi-romantic relationships: one with a six-foot-five-inch, two-hundred-twenty-pound Swedish musician whom I'll call Sven, a classmate in college; and one with a five-foot-nine-inch, one-hundred-forty-five-pound professor whom I'll call Mitch.

Sven lived downstairs and was into electropunk. He had dark eyes and pale skin, and he towered over me. He had a devastating sense of humor and became a member of the Pundits, a secret society of pranksters whose biggest contribution to campus life was throwing naked parties. He invited me to an Easter-themed naked party the spring of our junior year. When I arrived, he took out a tray of edible pastel body paint and wrote his name in all caps across my collarbone. A few nights later, he came over to watch a made-for-television movie about the show *Three's Company.* We dated for three weeks and never spoke again.

Mitch was a Jew from the Midwest who taught a popular introductory lecture course. A hundred students packed into his class—partly because his class satisfied a requirement for history majors and partly because Mitch was thirty-five and scrumptious. He wore thin wire-rimmed glasses on his boyish face, had a quick, easy smile and lips you could tell were warm and soft, even from the back of a large lecture hall. He called on me almost constantly in a class whose format did not involve a lot of people getting called on. He hand-graded my papers while teaching assistants handled everyone else's. Why me? I had no idea. We kissed once, at the end of a party in his apartment, when he sat down next to me on the couch and pounced. All I remember is that his breath tasted strongly of lox. Sometime shortly after I moved to New York, I got a press release from the Food Network saying he was scheduled to be a guest judge on *Iron Chef America.*

By then, I was already well into my plum $24,000-a-year gig at the *Observer.* I began in the vital capacity of "party reporter" and could not imagine there was anything more to want out of life. Every night I went somewhere different. There was the American Museum of Natural History dinner dance, where shiny-haired society ladies shimmied with their strong-chinned husbands underneath a life-size replica of a blue whale suspended from the ceiling. There was the cocktail party at *60 Minutes* correspondent Lesley Stahl's apartment uptown. There was a book party for celebrity wedding planner Preston Bailey at the Rainbow Room in Rockefeller Center. A long elevator ride carried a group of us up—everyone in suits and dresses, me in jeans, since I didn't own anything fancier—and on exiting, we were greeted by a long row of male models wearing nothing but cloth diapers, handing out chocolate-covered strawberries on sticks. The main room was decorated like Narnia, white lights dripping off enormous white-frosted trees. Two giant drag queens stood on pedestals, modeling jewel-encrusted wedding gowns. Preston Bailey had just done the Trump wedding—The Donald's third, to his model-wife Melania—and for a few minutes at least, Bailey was the toast of the town. A few weeks later, I paid two hundred dollars for my first designer dress, scrounged from the bottom of a cardboard box at a sample sale, which I bought to attend the premiere of the sixth season of *The Sopranos*. At the entrance, I stood for ten minutes watching celebrities and socialites smile for the cameras, performing their "step and repeat" on the red carpet in front of the gaggle of news photographers. I watched how the women turned just so to the most flattering angle and rested one hand on a hip, how they tipped their chins and half smiled. When I got home, I imitated it in the mirror, determined to discover my best side.

At first, I had no idea who any of these people were. I had none of the appropriate clothes for these parties. I was chubby because no one had introduced me to juice cleanses and Pilates mat classes yet, and I was awkward because I had never "socialized" before, I had simply worked and hung out with friends. Against such odds, a different person might have taken a different course. She might have said, "Forget this, I'm going to take my functioning brain, get a Ph.D. and do something meaningful with my life, like, I don't know, go fix cleft palates in Africa." What I thought, instead, was, "I want this." I want to be one of these people. I want to be glamorous and well dressed and smart and charming at parties. I want my hair to hang like a curtain. I want to be *successful in New York*, which was to say well-mannered and thin and stylish and talented at my work: "A comer," as former *Today* show anchor Jane Pauley once told me, when I interviewed her for a story. "A comer" was on the way up. "A goer" was on the way out. "A goer" was the thing I never wanted to be.

My entire world formed between these two poles. During work hours I studied New Yorkers, writing about the virtue of the comers and the hubris of the recently gone. After work, I did my best to approximate the life of a real city girl, rationing my salary among cheap gym classes, brown-rice sushi and discount designer clothes. I got makeup that complemented my skin tone and learned how to apply it. I cut my hair and straightened it and dyed it and developed a daily ritual of violence to keep it tame. I learned which clubs were worth going to and how to get into them. I talked about wine.

Did all of this make me happy?

Yes, it did.

I wish I wanted to fix cleft palates in Africa, but the truth is I wanted a glamorous life. I wanted life as it looked on the TV screen in my bedroom in Pittsburgh, when, as an awkward, nearsighted adolescent—cowinner of her middle school's pi-memorizing contest (we both got to seventy-five digits, which I can still recite by heart)—I dreamed of someday being a fancy New York City lady. Why were so many little girls around the country taken by this fantasy, which has been addictive in every incarnation but which became black-tar heroin in the form of *Sex and the City*? Why did we all want to be Carrie Bradshaw? She was a smart woman who used her talents to write a column about her sex life. She was single and basically useless. She kept company mostly with three other harpies, each as superficial as she, and they spent their time hopping from hot spot to hot spot, occasionally sleeping with losers. I had collected Susan B. Anthony dollars as a kid, cut out pictures of Gloria Steinem from magazines, listened to music by Stevie Nicks and made up songs about my favorite female astronaut, Sally Ride. I dressed up as Eleanor Roosevelt one year for a costume party at school. I worshipped journalist Linda Ellerbee, who hosted a television news program for kids; and inspired by her example, I once gave an exceedingly boring and earnest presentation to my sixth-grade classmates at the Ellis School for Girls about negative depictions of women in Procter & Gamble commercials.

So I was not a complete idiot. I was not underexposed to women of genuine merit. But still, above Eleanor Roosevelt, above Gloria Steinem, above Linda Ellerbee, I loved Carrie

Bradshaw. Here's why I thought I did: She was a commoner princess, an average-looking girl from nowhere special who had lots of pretty things and a steady supply of handsome boyfriends and a sexy job writing about her sexy life, and she'd achieved all this seemingly by her wits alone. I had a boring life in a dreary town. When I looked at what was missing, I saw pretty clothes, handsome boyfriends and sex. These were conspicuous voids and a lot easier to identify than "community, family and human connection," which Carrie Bradshaw also had, in her own strange, mostly silly way, and which I was also missing. But at that point, I didn't know those were things to miss.

Fix the outside; the inside will follow. This was the wrong lesson I learned from *Sex and the City*, and it's what I set out to do, as soon as I possibly could. I read about designer clothes. I learned how to walk in heels. I got my schnoz turned into a ski slope by a thin-fingered Pittsburgh plastic surgeon, who encouraged me to look through the magazines in his office and pick out which starlet I wanted to resemble. And when that was done, I turned my tiny nose up at the Midwest and made my way eventually to New York to be a journalist, just like Carrie—and Nora Ephron and Joan Didion and so many other women I worshipped—thereby inching ever closer to perfection.

In his essay "Toward an Understanding of the Messianic Idea in Judaism," Gershom Scholem, the founder of modern Kabbalistic scholarship, writes about what it means for people to spend their lives pursuing salvation. "There is something grand about living in hope," he writes, "but at the same time there is something profoundly unreal about it. It diminishes the singular worth of the individual, and he can never fulfill himself, because the incompleteness of his endeavors eliminates precisely what constitutes its highest value. Thus in Judaism the Messianic idea has compelled a *life lived in deferment*, in which nothing can be done definitely, nothing can be irrevocably accomplished."

In Pittsburgh, it was pretty much the same. The Messiah didn't come in high school, but Ben Johnson did once in my hair. The Messiah didn't come in college either, and he didn't come when I moved to New York because it wasn't just about moving there, it was about becoming that very specific person, having that precise life. Until I had that, no accomplishment was irrevocable. It was hard work, but I was up to it. Every pair of shoes, every clever turn of phrase, every new job was a step closer, and for a while it felt good to me to be moving toward a distant goal. A life lived in deferment is at least a productive one.

In his introduction to *The New Journalism*, a collection of literary nonfiction from the 1970s—"new journalism" described a style of reportage that read less like a newspaper column and more like a novel—Tom Wolfe describes the way he viewed his first reporting job in New York in the 1960s: as an amalgamation of first-reporting-job fantasies, forcibly rendered real. In his mind, it was Chicago in 1928; the hardbitten reporters worked only at night, only in between drinks and pee breaks in the Chicago River. Tom Wolfe's real first reporting job, for the *Springfield Union* in Massachusetts, was not quite so gritty. But what mattered was the childhood fantasy, not the small realities of actual life. Our first dreams grip us tightest and can refuse to let go. In some cases, that's a good thing—we need firemen and ballerinas, and Prince William did have to find a wife—but for the rest of us, it can be dangerous when you get lost in the details. "I wanted the whole movie," Wolfe writes, "nothing left out."

I also wanted the whole movie, and who cared if it was a bad movie (and an even worse sequel). I wish I had wanted to fix cleft palates, but for me there was only New York, and in New York, only journalism, a dying profession that pays no money, whose practitioners most people hate. Virtually any other career would have meant a faster path to riches, retirement, fulfillment of the soul. But journalism was the clear choice for a person like me, who wanted to be as close as possible to the center of things, who longed to be "part of the conversation." It is also the best job for people who are easily swept up in familiar story lines: the boy in the basket who floats down the river and becomes a king, the lonely little girl from Pittsburgh who goes to New York with high heels and a new nose and finds happiness. I have lived my entire life according to established story lines, even when they aren't true.

On September 15, 2006, with my movie life progressing according to plan, I went to a party in Prospect Heights, in the garden apartment of a magazine editor I'd never met. It was crowded and reeked of craft beer and midpriced cheese. When I walked in, I was drunk on three vodka sodas, wearing jeans bought that afternoon. I ran headlong into a handsome stranger. He made and held eye contact. Most of the party guests were saying their good-byes, beginning the long haul to the subway, to bed, to brunch the next morning. It was nearly three a.m.

The stranger was gorgeous. Tall, half-Israeli, with sharp features, green eyes and sleek designer clothes. He was hilarious. He was the perfect man for the girl I wanted to be. He was a high school rowing champion who'd once climbed Mount Rainier. His brother was whip smart, a future senator. His mother made delicious steamed halibut with white rice, asparagus and little sautéed cherry tomatoes. His father, a doctor, grew figs. He had a good job at a good law firm but dreamed of bigger things.

For our third date, he took me to see the Rolling Stones at Giants Stadium. He was the official on-call attorney for the concert, which struck me then as the sexiest thing a man could possibly be. Mick Jagger running across the stage had nothing on the tall, bright-eyed litigator with floor seats in the third row. He rented a white stretch limousine to take us to the show, and we laughed like rich teenagers on the way home, when he *bzzzzzzzzd* up the "privacy panel" as we sat, drinking champagne, draped across the rubbery blue leather seats. The first summer brought a trip abroad to Israel, to visit his family and the café where he'd once worked as a pastry chef, making legendary tiramisu. While there, we took a detour to Me'a She'arim, the neighborhood in northern Jerusalem where the ultra-Orthodox Jews live, where they may throw stones at you if you drive on shabbas or walk around in short sleeves. In the neighborhood's narrow, winding streets, I found and bought a children's toy called Memory Game. It was just like the one American kids play, where you try to match pairs of upside-down face cards by peeking at them two at a time and keeping track of who's where. Only these cards—forty in total—bore the faces of Talmudic scholars. The idea was to help young Hasids learn to distinguish between Menachem Mendel Schneerson and Shalom Dovber Schneersohn, for example. The problem with the game is that all twenty scholars look exactly alike: ancient white men with long beards and thick glasses, wild eyebrows, black hats and permanent scowls. It is the hardest children's game ever made. We took the game out at dinner parties, to make our secular Manhattan friends laugh.

The second year brought a rent-stabilized apartment in the West Village with a working fireplace we bragged about but never used. The third year brought a new apartment, bigger, on a sun-dappled cobblestoned street. I went from covering parties for the *New York Observer* to covering media for the *Wall Street Journal* to covering pop culture for the *Daily Beast*. Magazines flew me to Los Angeles and put me up at the Chateau Marmont to write profiles of movie stars, and sometimes he would come. Ours was a beautiful fairy-tale life. The sun was always shining, the skies were always blue and we were so ostentatiously pleased with our lot that, had this been a movie, it could suggest only one possible outcome: doom.

Doom

When I moved to one of the most religious communities in New York City, during one of the
darkest periods of my life, I didn't just casually
not believe in God. I passionately didn't believe in anything. I
didn't believe in peace, justice, Barack Obama or the Atkins
diet. I didn't believe in the power of song. I didn't believe the
Ronco Showtime rotisserie and BBQ oven could actually
cook a whole chicken in forty-five minutes, and I similarly,
but no more vehemently, didn't believe in the ultimate goodness of humanity. I thought there were two kinds of things in
the world: the known and the unknown. Love was chemicals
in the brain. Faith was fear. The chicken would cook in its own
goddamn time, and humanity was neither good nor bad: it
was a collection of particles arranged in the shape of people,
who lived for a while and then didn't.

I had never been a spiritual person. I had never been a

person particularly capable of faith. From the age of four, I remember being so terrified of my own mortality that it would keep me up at night, alone in our overheated house on our cul-de-sac. "What happens when you die?" I'd wonder, curled up in the center of my yellow gingham canopy bed, staring at the dancing dinosaur wall banner that ran along the ceiling edge. Deep down, even then, I knew: "Nothing. There is blackness and nothingness, and you never, ever, ever live again."

This refrain—"never, ever, ever again"—made me an early-age insomniac and a real pleasure at other kids' birthday parties. It's not that I was some marauding child goth. I was a cartoonishly girly little girl, small and dainty, ferrying constantly between piano lessons and ballet class, always wearing one of six or seven frilly pastel-colored Gunne Sax dresses. It just so happened that while all this was going on, I was also fixated on my own demise. My parents weren't exactly a comfort here. Both laboratory chemists—my father studied plastic, my mother rust—they worked long hours and spent their free time arguing about work or watching separate TVs on different floors of our house. I asked them once, "What happens when we die?" and in response they signed me up for Hebrew school, where I menaced the housewives who volunteered their Sunday mornings to be my introduction to "God."

God made no sense to me. The whole idea of Him struck me as awfully far-fetched. After my first few weeks at the ultra-Reform Temple Sinai, called St. Sinai by more righteous institutions in town, I quickly gave up asking questions and started acting out instead. One particularly dull day at Hebrew school, after I finished coloring in a Xeroxed picture of Moses carrying the Ten Commandments, I snuck into the school's administrative office, flipped on the PA system and, with all the strength of my eight-year-old vocal cords, gave voice to the Divine. "Hey, everyone!" I shouted into the live microphone. "God here." The plan was to dismiss class early, but before I could, I was tackled by my principal antagonist at St. Sinai, a third-grade teacher with a lazy eye, whom the kids secretly called Crossy. Crossy hauled me out by the collar of my shirt. I spent the next decade waiting out adulthood in those classrooms, sneaking out to smoke cigarettes in the parking lot and practicing my signature in the margins of my siddur. That one day on the PA system was about as close as I ever got to faith as a child, imitation my nearest form of piety.

In desperation, I started doing things that even then I recognized were ridiculous. My mother taught me to place fallen eyelashes on the tip of my finger and make a wish while blowing on them, like birthday candles. And so every time I lost an eyelash, I closed my eyes and blew and wished with all my heart that there really was a God, as if, were there not, one little girl huffing and puffing on dead cells would be enough to make it so. I resented my Christian classmates, with their Easter bunny and their Jesus and their big fat holiday hams. I had contempt for the girls who got into astrology in later years, who brought star charts to school and talked about how "everything happened for a reason" and how "the universe sends us signs." I did not believe the universe sent us signs. I did not believe we were in any kind of dialogue with the universe. I was the only child of two unhappy chemists. I believed in atoms, molecules and clinical depression.

The day after my thirteenth birthday, I had my bat mitzvah, becoming in the eyes of my people—but not, alas, in the eyes of anyone who could actually see—a fully realized Jewish woman. We Danas were not joiners, as a rule, and so even though we paid our Temple Sinai dues every year, and I dutifully went to Hebrew school and plodded through this holy rite, I hardly had a strong identity as part of a community of Jews. Given that there were only three of us, and we had a distant and cool relationship with my extended family, we were barely even part of a community of Danas. The Internet has made it so much easier to see how fungible community is in modern American life, now that we pass our time staring vacantly into bottomless social networks. But I lived a much more abstract, analog version of this as a kid, and even well into adulthood. While I was growing up, community meant almost nothing to me. It wasn't something I aspired to have, and it wasn't something I felt I missed. We went to Temple Sinai and I had my bat mitzvah not because of any stirrings of faith, nor any desire to be a part of something larger than ourselves, but because my parents were Jews, their parents before them were Jews, and doing these remedially Jewish things was what one had to do to continue considering oneself a Jew. It would have taken more effort to not do them. It's possible my parents are believers; we never discussed it. As a practical matter, we calibrated our level of participation in the traditions of the oldest organized religion in the world so as to cause minimal disturbance in the relentless march of history. Jews begat Jews begat Jews, who did certain things in the course of their lives because that's what everyone else had done in the long chain of begetting before them and would do in the endless future of begetting to come. Traditions, membership, participation at the minimal level: This was the path of least resistance.

The theme of my bat mitzvah, because everyone who was begat in the suburbs in the early 1980s had a theme, was "Reach for the Stars," since this blessed event fell in that tender period of youth after I attended Space Camp and before I discovered *Vogue*. For the nine years before I technically became a woman, I had pursued a course of study including typing, English, biology, field hockey, French, "kindness" and mathematics at my elementary school, a prim, secular institution with twenty-five students per grade. School was a mansion next to a Nabisco factory, which pumped out Nilla-wafer-scented air in giant puffs from a tall brick chimney, creating such a cloud of buttery sweetness around the little uniformed Ellis girls that looking back now, I have a distinct feeling of having grown up actually inside a cookie jar. These were happy years. I climbed trees. I got to be a Lost Boy in the school production of *Peter Pan*. I was a pain in the ass but smart and, against all odds, not totally unpopular.

The summer before my eighth-grade year, when the holy bat mitzvah was to take place, I spent yet another eight agonizing weeks at Kutsher's Sports Academy. Kutsher's was a camp for lunky, heathen Jewish youth, and it took place near an old, deserted *Dirty Dancing*–style resort in the Catskills. I'd found it advertised in the back of the *New York Times Magazine*, and in some fit of delusion, had begged my parents to go. See, I liked sports, and there "sports" were, right in the title! What a moron I was. A Klan retreat would have been more nurturing. Why did I keep going after the first miserable summer? Because every camper who made it through three summers got a free T-shirt, featuring the contemptible institution's hideous logo, typically rendered in navy blue, but done instead in an elite, VIP, super-exclusive navy blue *plaid*. It was the purple heart of camp shirts, and I had to have it. By my third year at Kutsher's, though nothing much had improved, I had at least settled into my nickname—"Dictionary," so given because I'd skipped a grade in math during my first summer there and had stupidly kept an algebra textbook hidden under my bed. My torturer/bunkmates found they needed something to yell after they'd ripped off my towel and begun chasing me naked around the flagpole in the center of girls' camp, a Kutsher's pastime, and forgoing accuracy for expediency, they chose "Dictionary." It was zippier than "Algebra: Structure and Method, Book I."

By Summer Three, every girl was studying for her bat mitzvah. I had no interest in memorizing Hebrew words I didn't understand, set to a tune my tone-deaf vocal cords couldn't follow anyway. By then I had discovered a better prophet: J. D. Salinger. I hid his books, beginning with *Catcher in the Rye*, then on to the Glass stories, one after another, inside the Xerox copies of my Torah portion, pretending to study any moment I could. Holden Caulfield was fine, but the Glass family was a revelation. I had no idea what any of them was talking about, but the words rolled around in my head like marbles, heavy and smooth. I hadn't realized families could be like this. That summer, I wanted nothing so much as a single bed in a cramped Upper West Side apartment loaded to the brim with prodigies. I wanted parents in vaudeville and my own spot on a radio show for precocious youngsters. Most pressingly, I wanted to know what happened to perfect Seymour, my dream man, after his wedding day. I didn't find out until I got home, six weeks later, because a little soccer-playing harridan named Jessica discovered *Nine Stories* under my bed one day and doused it in the shower.

When I returned to Pittsburgh that fall, Temple Sinai's spiritual leader, Rabbi Toby, was not pleased with my lack of progress. I haven't always been great with authority, and I regarded this man, with his Brillo-pad hair and the oblong black mole in the center of his cheek, as a petty dictator. I had never heard Hebrew spoken by an Israeli, but even still I could tell his pronunciation was fake. I winced at how prayers seemed to shoot from the back of his throat like Ping-Pong balls. "What kind of a sanctimonious asshole do you have to be to become a *rabbi*?" I used to think, but this was before I moved in with one.

My Haftorah portion had something to do with the coming of the Messiah.

"When do you think the Messiah will come?" Rabbi Toby asked one afternoon in his cavernous office, which had deep purple carpeting, slate paneled walls and a vast dark cherry wood desk. Many American synagogues have adopted this aesthetic, favoring a heavy, windowless design over anything with natural light, giving a visitor the feeling of tunneling her way to God. Where most churches reach skyward, with big, ostentatious lofted beams and towering windows, the average shul tries not to draw attention. It is short and squat—not entirely unlike the average shul-goer—an inverted, eggplant-colored bunker just one or two stories above the earth. Architecturally, Reform Judaism is the stalagmite of religions. As the poet James Merrill, another of my adolescent WASP heroes, might say, it's less of a lofty spiritual pursuit, more of a *mauve*ment.

"I don't know," I told Rabbi Toby, avoiding his eyes. Finally, I peered up and met his disappointed gaze. "Soon?"

He shook his head. He had just explained to me everything that would need to happen before the Messiah came. There would have to be no more war, no more hate, no more ugliness in men's hearts.

"Not soon?" I tried again.

"Not for a very long time," he replied, using a whisper-soft voice to convey gravity. I briefly allowed myself the fantasy of flinging a whipped-cream pie in his face.

In fact, Jewish teaching allows two very different conditions for the coming of the Messiah. One scenario, preferred by Rabbi Toby and the drivers of mitzvah tanks everywhere, is the triumph of virtue among men. The other scenario is the triumph of vice, "redemption through sin," as Scholem called it, where the entire world turns into Sodom and Gomorrah, full of war and hatred and rampant anal sex. Given all this, it strikes me that "Soon?" is not a terrible answer to a question about the timing of the apocalypse.

MY THERAPIST IN NEW YORK IS a stunning half-Jewish, half-Italian woman whom I'll call Madeleine. She is unmarried, drives an orange Vespa and works out of the most perfect office in Manhattan, with wood floors, a vaulted ceiling and a garden growing outside the windows that is so wild it seems on the verge of breaking in. She is exactly the person I would pick for a mother or a sister if you got to pick, which in New York, for enough money, you kind of do. Madeleine says that when a person is preoccupied with thoughts of death, it usually means something in that person's life is passing away, since we are all in a constant process of living and dying, of casting off skins. It makes sense, then, that when you are a kid, when everything is compressed, when the gradient of life is so quick and clear—What *doesn't* change in the course of nine months of grade school?—that an awareness of loss might haunt you. As I got older, I began to notice the fear would lift for a time, when I was busy with a school play or infatuated with some boy. Then, like flu season, it would return, inevitable in times of transition and often, frustratingly, at moments in life when I was supposed to be happiest.

During what I didn't then know were the final months of my perfect relationship, I could not get my mind off one particular imagined scene, which played itself in a loop behind my eyes: I am sitting in a white paper dressing gown on the edge of a tall examining table in a doctor's office. The backs of my thighs are stuck to the plastic cushion, and I lift them one at a time, listening to the sound and feeling the rubber-band sting of each coming unstuck. It is freezing in the dry, antiseptic room, and I stare at my toes. The red nail polish is chipping. They are blue from the cold. Somewhere outside my field of vision, like the nanny in the *Muppets*, a doctor speaks. I miss the exact words but gather the gist: cancer (or whatever). "You're dying."

It got so I was swallowing sleeping pills every night to knock myself out before the fatal-diagnosis vision could creep into my thoughts. When my perfect boyfriend and I smoked pot, which we were doing a lot of then, I would think about not thinking about it, stoner style, and it was the closest I got to relief. Many months later, I was curled up on someone else's big plush couch, watching a movie one Sunday night, and my heart nearly stopped when I saw a version of the scene play out on-screen: It was not the universe talking to me after all, it was the Coen Brothers, and the doctor visit occurred at the beginning of *A Serious Man*. But at the time, it was a mystery, an assertive, irritating, frightening nuisance. I told Madeleine about the vision, and she said, "Maybe something in your life is dying."

"Hmm," I said, pretending to consider the idea. This is a woman whose every word was gospel for me, but at the time, it seemed awfully fruity. What could be dying? I had a great job, a great apartment, a great everything.

And then one night in the middle of October, when I was

still telling myself a story of uninterrupted bliss, my perfect West Village apartment flooded. I am not a biblical scholar, but I've read a lot of bad books and watched a lot of terrible movies in my life, and I know a heavy-handed metaphor when I see it. Before the flood, things were already chipping away in the sweet sunlit home we shared. Our tiny galley kitchen, with its painted-over French window, had already been overrun by cockroaches. A growing patch of ceiling in the hallway had long ago started to wither and crack, so there was a low-grade fake snowstorm every time one of us entered or left, like cheap special effects. But it wasn't until I found myself stranded in the middle of our queen-size bed, with water pouring in from a gaping hole in the roof, that I had the first inkling that something more filmic was going on. My home was collapsing around me.

I was beginning the fourth year of my relationship with Chad, whose name was not Chad, but let's go with that. Chad was on an airplane at the time. Through what was then a miracle of modern technology, he was connected to the Internet from his coach seat. But what could he do? A monsoon was raging over New York City and he was gazing out at a clear night, thirty-two thousand feet above Nebraska. I put out all the pots and pans we had and was emptying them frantically, one after another, while thunder and lightning, so violent they seemed canned, exploded outside the windows. It was midnight, and our superintendent wasn't answering the phone. "Did you lay out the beach towels?" he typed from up there in the clouds. Yes, I had. Here we were, living in the future, connected by satellites and fiber-optic cables and all the other filaments people have built to hold each other close even when they're far, and it was all useless. "Try the super again," he typed. I didn't bother.

Instead I waited up for Chad to get home that night and ran into his arms when he arrived. He brought me a box of chocolates, and I dropped down on the couch and ate one self-consciously, then wanted another but didn't have it. A damp mass of beach towels, brown with dirt and smelling like clay, sat in a heap in the bathtub. I could hear the roaches tap-tap-tapping around on the floor of the kitchen. The storm had passed, but it had been devastating, knocking down power lines around the city, destroying 508 trees in Central Park. If there is a God, he's a bad director, unsubtle and obtuse.

After the flood—after the cockroaches descended and the ceiling caved in and the Hudson River turned to blood—did I then stop for a moment to consider whether Someone might be trying to tell me something? Of course not. There is no Someone, and there was nothing to tell. A few weeks later, I packed a bag and flew to the Middle East, to attend a film festival in Doha, Qatar, a fake, empty city baking on the west coast of the Persian Gulf, an hour south of Baghdad. The trip was a boondoggle, arranged through work, with all expenses paid. I had my own room at the Four Seasons, overlooking the hazy blue water and a small makeshift beach built exclusively for visiting Westerners, since locals are forbidden from sunbathing. The room was decorated in mildewed floral fabrics with not a hint of Arab influence. When I closed the heavy brocade curtains and looked around in the yellow lamplight, I could imagine I was visiting a wealthy aunt somewhere, if I'd had a wealthy aunt somewhere, instead of what I was actually doing, which was biding time in the middle of the desert while my life back home continued its biblical demise.

The business-class flight back to New York was my last innocence. I sipped soup and watched romantic comedies I would never otherwise have bothered to see and nibbled on an Ambien to drift in and out of sleep in my horizontal chair. I didn't know if we were allowed to keep the fancy pajamas they handed out for the flight so I hid them in my suitcase before we landed. I made friends with a Mormon woman, a mother of three who lived in the suburbs. We took our picture standing in the aisle, and I bragged to her about my great boyfriend, and we planned to have dinner together someday soon. I brought Chad two presents: a T-shirt from the Four Seasons lobby gift shop that had three rough sketches of donkeys and the slogan "Particularity Qatar!" and a plastic mujahideen, a children's toy, that lit up via an on/off switch located directly above the animal's visible rectum.

Four days later I was sitting in the living room of my crumbling apartment, dizzy from lack of sleep, staring at the man of my crumbling life and finding myself unable to catch his eye. The Particularity Qatar! shirt was long forgotten on the couch. What had happened, exactly? I wasn't sure. While I was gone there had been a wild Halloween night and a flirtation— chaste, he swore with a filmmaker named Christy. I found

out, I left, I cried, I returned, and here we were, sitting opposite each other, not drinking a bottle of red wine. I remember
little about how the fight began and less about how it pro-
gressed. What I recall most clearly about the whole ordeal is
the point at which my brain and body split apart and began
operating separately and in opposition.

Things with Chad had been difficult for a while—for how
long, I refused to contemplate. Our life was still perfect, of
course, except that he had slipped out of his law firm job
about nine months into our relationship and had languished
around the apartment, spending days surfing the Internet in
his underwear, hammering out breathless essays on obscure
topics, which disappeared into the lukewarm soup of the
Internet immediately after he published them, for free, on the
Huffington Post. He was drinking a lot, staying out late,
sleeping into the middle of the afternoon. And he increasingly found greater fault with me: I didn't dance well. I read
too much. Couldn't I be thinner, stand up straighter, wear
more makeup and higher heels? Of course, there are two
sides to every story, and if Chad was offered the chance to
defend himself, I'm sure he'd come up with something, probably something breathless and obscure that he would publish
for free on the *Huffington Post.* For now, you'll just have
to accept that my version of things is correct. If I may
speak objectively, it is not only correct but also quite generous
to Chad.

So Chad had had a "platonic" fling with Christy the filmmaker, but he was very sorry about that and also about all the

mean things he'd said about my dancing and my posture. He would fix everything if I would just stay. He wanted me to be his wife. I would never find "compatibility" like this any-where else, he said. I would never find anyone who could make me laugh like he could. There was just one issue from his perspective, one small detail, but he vowed we could work through it. He called this "our chemistry problem." The issue was: I wasn't pretty enough.

"But with Randi and Jacob"—these were our friends, on whose couch I'd been sleeping since the fight began—"he just thinks she's beautiful all the time," I sputtered, "when she's tired and cranky, when she hasn't showered for three days, when she doesn't feel beautiful at all." I stopped and looked at him, but he refused my eyes. "Do you ever think I'm beautiful?"

He said nothing for an outrageously long period of time, and this is when my brain walked out and my body stayed put. At last he looked up, slowly shrugged his shoulders, raised his hands in the air in a gesture of hopelessness and said, with regret, "I think you're pretty?" Like that—"pretty?"—as if he were apologizing for putting too much salt in the mashed potatoes.

I spent a long time staring into my full glass of wine. I felt like a kid safety-belted into the backseat of a car, looking out the window at the scenery whizzing by and unable to focus on a single image. What do you do when the person you love most in the world confirms all your worst fears? All my fixing things from the outside had failed. Everything I had ever wanted—New York, the great apartment, the glamorous job, the perfect boyfriend, the shiny hair—felt like a sham.

"Why did you ask me out in the first place?" I said at last through tears, gripping the stem of the glass.

"You were cute?" he asked after a minute. Everything was a question. "I don't know?"

His past girlfriends had been "beautiful on the outside," he said. I was "beautiful on the inside," an observation that should have left me more comforted than it did. He itemized the features of my body that were under par, physical attributes that hadn't quite worked for him from the start and had only marginally improved over the years. His skin looked gray to me from across the room. Deep, dark bags hung under his eyes. He had bought a new-model iPhone that afternoon, when I had been riding around aimlessly on subway trains, crying behind black sunglasses. The torn white Apple packaging made a halo around him. His posture was that of an old man, but the scene conjured a little boy on Christmas Day. Tears streamed from his eyes.

I felt a wave of nausea and stumbled off to the bathroom, but he intercepted me in the hall, pressing his forehead into my shoulder. To me, he was perfect looking, tall and broad, "a Maccabee," as I told my friends. I never quite understood how this man, who had been so popular in high school, who had lost his virginity to an older girl at the age of thirteen and had had women (and men) throwing themselves at him ever since—how he could possibly fall in love with me: the late bloomer, the nerd, the girl who had lost her virginity just to be rid of it at the age of twenty-three. Truth be told, he never quite understood it either. But it had happened, and it had felt powerfully inescapable—exactly right—for a long time. Now, all of a sudden, it didn't.

We stood frozen in the hallway for what seemed like hours that night, crying and saying nothing. It was late, so eventually we went to bed. He tried to hold me, but I wouldn't let him. Instead I curled up on the far edge of the mattress that a few weeks earlier had been my life raft, feeling hideous and unlovable. A short time later, I woke to the sound of Chad sobbing upright next to me. "I don't want this to be our last night together," he said when he caught his breath. It was.

The next morning we went to get breakfast and didn't eat it. I wondered what to do with my laundry. Where did it go if not in the laundry bag with the rest of our things? He pleaded with me to combine our clothes, as if one last trip to ABC Cleaners would be the thing to wring this misery out. I told him I thought we needed to be apart for a while. "Okay," he said. "You take five years and go sow your wild oats and then you'll come back and be my wife."

It was a beautiful day outside, bright and cool with a light breeze. I sat down on our bed and straightened my legs, pressing the backs of my thighs against the corner of the mattress. It felt dry and cool inside the antiseptic room. Chad came in and sat down next to me. "I have something to tell you," he said. I stared down at my feet. The red nail polish was chipping. My toes were turning blue from the cold. From somewhere out of my field of vision, Chad spoke. I couldn't quite make out the words, but I gathered the gist: He'd cheated.

With strangers. Without condoms. While drunk and high. For going on three months now. While I was working. While I was off at yoga class or waiting for him to come home. Remember that time right before my birthday, when I'd had a rough day at work and he'd told me not to think about a thing, that he'd bought salmon and asparagus and was going to make me a special dinner? I'd come home and found the apartment empty, the salmon still wrapped in its protective paper, the asparagus in plastic, uncooked. He called to say he was still at a party, having such a good time, couldn't he just stay a little longer? Sure, I said, whatever you want. I got into bed to read a few pages of my book and nodded off eventually. He came in at one o'clock in the morning, woke me up, showered and made me a fried egg on dry toast. I found out later she was one of those insufferably flawless exotic goddesses who somehow abound in New York. I found this out because he'd posed with his arm around her for a society photographer, and I came across the picture at work. The first thing I recognized was my scarf around his neck.

He kept talking. but I didn't hear a word. I just focused my eyes on my fading pedicure. Taking pity at last, my brain came back for my body, a searchlight cutting through the fog. "This relationship is over," I said. "Please leave so I can pack my things."

He didn't move.

I am the child of screamers. The sound of screaming makes
my stomach clench and my head hurt. It makes me fold up
into a ball, search out the nearest blanket to hide beneath. I
had never screamed, not once, in my adult life. Until that
moment. Just then, my cheeks caught fire, my lungs inflamed,
and it suddenly felt like there weren't enough *fuck*s in the universe. From a safe distance, I saw the whole scene play out, as
if I were back on Qatar Airways, drinking curried broth and
half watching the latest Sandra Bullock flick between naps.
All I consciously felt in the moment was a righteous thumping in my chest, the timpani drumbeat of a woman in love
with a man, in love with her life, with the look of her life—
scorned and humiliated.

I told him I would never be his wife, never have his children, that he was pathetic and would never be happy and
would probably die alone. He shuffled out into the hall. I tried
to slam the door, but because of the water damage it no longer
fit its frame and came shuddering back open a couple of
inches. The violence of the gesture caused a cascade of white
paint chips to tumble down from the decomposing spot on
the ceiling, narrowly missing his head. I could see his face
looking in at me, while I stood there shaking.

I screamed until my throat gave out. And then, as quickly
as the rage had come, it left me. My hands shook as I packed
T-shirts, jeans, sweaters, underwear, laptop, chargers, contact
lenses and all the other basic necessities. Chad stood in the living room, staring at the ground. I walked past him in silence,

out the door and down the four flights of stairs into the crisp, brilliant afternoon.

He caught up to me just as I was turning north on Eighth Avenue. It had been a two-block sprint, and he was winded. He stopped in front of me, panting, struggling to catch his breath.

"What," I said, not as a question. He was blocking my way.

Because it was a gorgeous late fall day, everyone in the West Village was out for a stroll, sucking up the last ultraviolet rays before hunkering down for a long cold winter. Chad and I, standing at an angry distance on the sidewalk, were a boulder in a stream. I saw the crowds flowing around us and felt a sharp pang of envy. For one thing, their lives weren't coming crashing down in this instant, as far as I could tell. For another, they were getting a show. One of the single best features of life in Manhattan is that occasionally you'll chance upon a public breakup. You hear them from time to time, out on the street or in the apartment down the hall, a woman screaming and a man issuing grunts in his own defense, or the other way around. It's free theater, better than Broadway. Voices will sink to low, furious tones outside a bar at two a.m.; paint chips will tumble from the ceiling above. Poor breathless Chad and I were collapsing dramatically, in full public view. If anyone noticed, they didn't let on. But New Yorkers are used to this sort of thing. We are people who build towers and then spend our lives climbing them. When it all falls apart here, it *falls*.

Chad slumped over, one hand on his waist.

I realize now, looking back, how lucky I am. Some people agonize for years after a breakup, driven mad by ambivalence and longing. I had it easy. In that moment, watching this person I no longer recognized struggle to collect himself, I felt something pull and snap into place inside me, some unknown internal override mechanism taking control of my system, steeling my stomach, propping me up, clearing my eyes. At my feet was everything I'd ever wanted. Instead of falling down with it, I floated away.

Lush Places

The *Daily Beast* offices are on 18th Street and the West Side Highway in the Chelsea neighborhood of Manhattan, on the second floor of an all-glass building designed by Frank Gehry to evoke a ship's billowing sails. Inside, the decor seems to have been provided by the makers of Skittles, with red, yellow, green and blue contemporary furniture dotting the open floor plan. The result is a futuristic Scandinavian-style work space, where you might expect to find tall pretty blondes in tight sheath dresses walking around with trays of protein shakes. The lights are large disks suspended from the ceiling. The bathrooms are covered in red, yellow, blue, green and purple wall tiles, with automatic sinks and toilets that go on and off with little warning or provocation.

My title at the *Beast* was senior correspondent. That work entailed reporting the occasional bit of breaking news, but it mostly meant I wrote topical essays intellectualizing tabloid news stories, or attempting to, drawing traffic without reveling too much in the muck. The day Chad met the insufferably flawless exotic goddess, for example, I happened to have written a piece called "The Immaculate Confession," in which I praised late-night talk show host David Letterman for the candor he'd used in discussing his much-publicized extramarital affairs.

Working at the *Beast* was my dream job, one of those fakeseeming Manhattan gigs that require one to attend fashion shows and posh luncheons at our editor's brownstone on Sutton Place. On one occasion, I spent an evening chatting with Meryl Streep. On another, I gave Madeleine Albright a hug. The *Beast* itself was a bubble, secure and insular at a time when virtually every other news organization was suffering through painful cutbacks. Of course, it is always more complicated than that, and the *Beast* didn't remain insular and safe forever. Any workplace, especially a media organization and especially one as small and quirky as the *Beast*, is full of drama and intrigue. But when I squint my eyes and look back on my first year there, I just see rainbows after the flood.

The *Beast* was named after the fictional paper in Evelyn Waugh's comedic novel *Scoop*. Its entire staff was comprised of fictional-seeming characters, led by our indefatigable, brilliant, warmhearted, blond and terrifying editor in chief, journalism legend Tina Brown. Tina was a grown-up publishing prodigy, now in her fifties and several acts into her career. She had been the editor in chief of *Tatler*, the glamorous British fashion and news magazine, when she was twenty-five years old. She went on to edit *Vanity Fair* and *The New Yorker* and to launch a magazine called *Talk*, which was more famous for its largesse than anything else—for the enormous, star-studded parties thrown in its honor—but which was done in by the economic realities of post–September 11 New York. Like any woman who attains a position of power by means other than angelic sweetness (which is how precisely no woman attains a position of power), Tina came to be known by an easy carica-ture: manic, relentless, willing to do anything to make her magazines sell. This portrait is reductive, unfair and also, in the best sense, true. She was a visionary editor, curious to the point of exhaustion, and her staff spent most of its time trying to channel her editorial sensibilities into the perfect mix of high high culture and low low. Like many of my colleagues, I regarded her with a mix of worshipful devotion and fear.

As the recession drove away advertisers and the Internet slowly tortured and killed off print media, we floated along in our Gehry boat, far from making a profit but still, by the grace of our wealthy owner Barry Diller, blissfully unaffected. The building was loaded up with free goodies: all the candy, chips, yogurt, sodas, energy bars, carrot sticks, pudding and Jell-O you could eat. Each floor had Wii video game con-soles, large flat-panel televisions, and cabinets filled with any kind of medication you might want for anything that ailed you. Chalkboard paint covered the walls, and we were encour-aged to draw on them. A Wellness Room on the ninth floor, complete with massage chair and suede couch, was available any time you felt like dozing off. A restaurant-quality espresso machine made perfect soy lattes at the push of a button, and every Friday we had brunch. There were about thirty of us at the *Beast* when I got there, and my colleagues all struck me as impossibly hip and brainy. We spent a lot of time sitting around drinking lattes and eating bagels, talking about what was going on in the world and trying to make each other laugh.

A typical day at the office began around nine, with oatmeal and a scan through the morning's papers and blogs. Then came an editorial meeting at eleven, where we talked about the big news stories of the day and how we should cover them, and after that, lunch. In the afternoon I exchanged a trickle of instant messages with journalist friends, made phone calls to sources and, most days, wrote or edited a story. It wasn't heart surgery, but it was humane and periodically satisfying work. I covered media and fashion and a little bit of everything else. I mostly liked the people in these industries, so it hardly felt like work to call them up and chat. But after Chad kicked in the ground floor of my house of cards, this work felt not only unworklike but also soul-crushingly pointless and banal. The same person who had wanted him had wanted this. It was all born of the same fantasy, and that fantasy was stupid and wrong. My only recourse was to have some oatmeal and stare into space.

Work became impossible in the wake of my breakup, when the war between my body and brain still raged. My body wanted Chad, to hug him, to hide in his arms and disappear back into my old easy life. My brain was constantly performing an autocorrect on this impulse, putting those arms in their proper context: wrapped around other girls. This mechanism produced a kind of seasickness, a lolling back and forth between head and heart that caused me to stumble around the big glass building, struggling to hold my free Gatorade down.

Chad and I broke up on a Saturday, and I went to stay with Randi and Jacob in their stylish one-bedroom apartment in Brooklyn. Jacob was a record producer at the label that had discovered Hasidic rapper Matisyahu. Randi was a pint-size prop stylist and a former editor at *Martha Stewart Weddings*. She had a lovely trilling laugh and walked around in hot pink neoprene sneakers with little slots for each of her toes. Jacob couldn't take his eyes off her. They met one year on Halloween when he dressed up as a bathroom wall and she wrote her phone number on him. Their life since seemed like one perpetual Martha Stewart wedding. Their library was arranged in rainbow order and every morsel of food they ate was beautiful and cooked from scratch. I always half expected to find a photographer huddled in the bathroom, artfully shooting their stunning array of soaps. I shared their couch with Olive, their Boston terrier, who humped my leg before bed each night but who otherwise was a warm and welcome presence in the days immediately following the collapse of my entire life.

I was shocked that I could still walk and breathe those days, but discovered I was useless at most other things. On my way to work on Monday, I stopped off at the drugstore and, twenty minutes after entering, found myself in a Hamlet-like paralysis before a wall of deodorants. I read the ingredients lists, compared unit prices and still couldn't decide. I imagined myself growing old in the aisle, gumming oatmeal, acquiring cats. Finally I settled on a stick of Degree that promised to be "Extra Responsive in Emotional Moments!*" I followed the asterisk to the fine print: "*releasing sweat." I applied my extra-responsive deodorant in the bathroom of my doctor's office, where I went for a quick STD test before lunch. ("Afraid of needles?" the nurse asked as I sobbed on the examining table. "Yes," I lied.) A few days later the results came back—clean. So there was that to be thankful for.

In the mail that day—in a Federal Express envelope marked Urgent—came a galley for a book called *Hunting Season: A Field Guide for Targeting and Capturing the Perfect Man*, which arrived from the publisher's publicity office. I flipped to the first chapter. "Open season on men begins on April 1 and ends on September 30," it said, under a picture of a rifle and a pair of binoculars. I sank lower in my chair, pulled on my headphones and called up an old episode of *Doogie Howser, M.D.* on the computer at my desk. This was my favorite television show in middle school, before evil Carrie Bradshaw and her coven of witches stole my brain. The episode I watched was called "Breaking Up Is Hard to Doogie." In it, the child-prodigy doctor and his high school girlfriend, Wanda, mutually decide to break up one night at a dance. Everything goes peacefully and amicably. No one ends up homeless, crashing temporarily on their gorgeous friends' restored vintage couch while a female Boston terrier humps her leg at night. I wished then, as fervently as ever, that life were more like nineties sitcoms.

After Doogie typed his usual pat diary entry on the old Macintosh IIe, I turned back to Craigslist, determined to sally forth into single life in similarly calm fashion. I sallied for a good thirty seconds before the nausea returned, sending me staggering off to the candy-colored bathroom. I had moved six times in the previous five years. More of my earnings had gone to FlatRate Moving than to my 401(k)—in fact, I had contributed nothing to my 401(k)—and much of what was left went to clothes, shoes and other necessities I deemed necessary, like bimonthly trips to Kim, a petite Japanese stylist who spent three hours bleaching every last shred of pigment from my hair. I didn't have a savings account or a credit card for my first five years in New York. Whatever money I earned flowed right through Citibank, without slowing to gather a penny of interest, and landed somewhere on my body. It was a glorious waterfall of consumption, the sort of thing you only see on-screen, when the characters don't have to think about retirement or medical emergencies or anything beyond the final credits.

My lack of financial planning acumen, plus heartbreak, made for less than ideal apartment hunting conditions when the time came to start from scratch. But there I was, trolling a site better known for abetting serial murder than functional roommate couplings. The first place I found that I could afford was advertised under the headline "$650 KOSHER kitchen."

It was available immediately and required no commitment. The post mentioned a preference for a male roommate. "Would you consider a girl?" I wrote and then made a halfhearted boast about my cooking skills. The reply came back immediately. I got it on my BlackBerry, curled up on the floor of the handicapped stall.

hi!
sure, come on by.
cosmo

Cosmo gave me detailed directions to his apartment, which was in a part of Brooklyn that seemed so remote it might as well have been Vermont. I wonder if this person will murder me, I thought as I boarded the number 3 train, not caring terribly much one way or the other. Across the aisle was an advertisement for Dallas BBQ's brand-new "sticky wings," which were pictured steaming, on a plate, in grotesque, magnified detail. For the duration of the ride, I struggled to keep the meager contents of my stomach down.

I emerged from the subway and careened toward a public trash can. When I recovered my bearings, such as they were, I found myself staring up at 770 Eastern Parkway, the enormous Gothic red-brick building that is the international headquarters of the Lubavitch movement. This is where the great Menachem Mendel Schneerson, seventh and final Grand Rebbe of the Lubavitch sect of ultra-Orthodox Jews, had lived for more than half a century. The headquarters, known inside the community just as "770," is dark and towering. Stiffly dressed men enter and exit at all times. I recognized the building instantly because although this was my first trip to Crown Heights, I'd seen it before: Lubavitchers have built exact replicas in Jerusalem and Sydney. The Jerusalem version is a red-brick anomaly in a city infrastructure made of sparkling, ivory-colored Jerusalem stone—an impossible waiver and one only a community as powerful as the Lubavitchers could obtain. I visited it with Chad; and someone told us the idea behind the replicas was to ensure that Schneerson wouldn't feel lost if, in returning to earth to redeem humanity, he happened to land somewhere other than Brooklyn. We thought the whole thing was hilarious. If he's the *Messiah*, how could he possibly get lost?

Brooklyn is to the south and east of Manhattan. To get there by subway, one travels down the center of the island, underneath tourist-clogged Soho, posh Tribeca, the tiny harried alleys of Wall Street and the East River. Yuppies, yoga teachers, food co-op volunteers and literary editors have colonized many acres of the northwest portion of Brooklyn, but at the time I moved there, they had not yet reached Crown Heights. Still, the distance separating that neighborhood from the heart of Manhattan was only a few miles. It had taken me thirty minutes, at rush hour, to get to Kingston Avenue, which by all outward signs was located somewhere in eighteenth-century Russia. En route to Cosmo, I passed through a gauntlet of quaint local businesses that cater to the ultra-Orthodox community: Mendy's Delicatessen, Rebecca Wigs, Crown Hot

Bagels, Boytique (with miniature tallit "for your lil' rebbe"), Merkaz Stam Religious Articles, Weinstein's Hardware and Houseware, the offices of Avroham Popack attorney at law, Judaica World, the offices of Alan Newark ("podiatrist and foot specialist"), Hamafitz Stam ("The source for Torah and tefillin") and, of course House of Glatt ("We continue to serve the Chabad community with kashrut, quality, service and honesty"). There were also the school buildings on every corner: double, triple, quadruple endowed, their benefactors' names emblazoned in giant type across their plain brick exteriors. On the way, I passed three Hasidic beggars standing open-palmed outside a synagogue, accepting change from the Lubavitcher ladies hurrying by. When I walked by, the homeless men put their hands in their pockets.

Bernice Court, at 621 Crown Street, was six long blocks from 770. The entrance to the apartment building was through a heavy double-locked metal gate, which opened into a vast arched foyer. The interior design was neo-everything, with immense Doric columns painted gray and mauve; elaborate ivory-colored crown molding; and nooks made to hold small marble statues, which had either been stolen or, more likely, never existed. It smelled strongly of Lemon Pledge and cigarettes, as if a local prison cleaning crew had just made the rounds.

Cosmo met me at the bottom of the stairs, said a curt hello and didn't offer to shake my hand. He wore a T-shirt covered in Chinese characters with his *tzitzit*, the strings of his religious garment, hanging out beneath the hem. We walked up the three flights to the apartment in silence, and then as soon as he let me in, he went straight to the kitchen and began washing dishes. "Your room is in the back," he said.

The first thing I noticed about the apartment was the smell, which hovered like a storm cloud over the front door. Part biological, part chemical, with base notes of dead animal and burned rubber, the message it sent was not "Welcome home!" but "Run." But for whatever reason—exhaustion, and also not caring about anything anymore—I didn't run. There were two old bicycles right in front of the door, along with a large table covered in upturned black top hats and unreturned Blockbuster VHS tapes. Holding my nose, I squeezed past.

"Do you need a bicycle?" Cosmo called from the kitchen.

His bedroom was on the left, the kitchen was on the right and before me was a vast living room, as large as any I'd ever seen in New York. The windows were wide open, and the chilly air only made it seem emptier and more cavernous. I made my way to "my room," which was on the other side of the living room, directly across from the bathroom. I flipped on the lights. The room was bigger than my entire former apartment, with wood floors and ivory walls, high ceilings and ornate detailing. Once, many years ago, it must have been beautiful. By the time I got there, it was a repository for abandoned kitsch, as if a whole series of people had stopped by briefly, during a hectic period in their lives, and then ditched the place, leaving their strangest or most useless possession behind. By the time I arrived, the room boasted a half-destroyed armoire with a bobblehead statue of Princess

Leia, a three-legged coffee table from the 1970s that held an old record player and two giant Aiwa speakers, a stack of jazz records that appeared to have been used as knife sharpeners, and a kooky blue-and-yellow-patterned knit yarmulke.

The walls were thin enough that I could hear the couple next door screaming at each other but thick enough that I couldn't make out what they were shouting about. They screamed like that, almost without interruption, favoring the early morning and late night hours, for the next nine months— and I never knew why. I went to the window, over which someone had mounted a not-small American flag. I lifted up the glass and peered out. My room looked over a parking lot where the Lubavitchers kept some of their mitzvah tanks. Half a dozen sat in a neat row, God's battalion at rest. "The view is the best part," said Cosmo, hovering in the doorway.

We sat for a minute and talked. Mostly, he talked. "Sex, booze and cigarettes are cool with me," he said. "I don't care what you do in there." I nodded. "Drugs are not allowed." Okay. "All I really care about is that you can pay the rent on time—and by on time I mean, like, within ten days of the start of the month." Okay. "The last guy was a real mother-fucker about the rent, and I do not want to deal with that again." It grew dark out, and Cosmo offered to walk me to the train. Jews make up about 10 percent of the residents of Crown Heights, according to the last census. The other 90 percent are West Indian immigrants. En route to the subway, we went a different way than I'd come, up Troy Avenue, through the West Indian neighborhood.

"Is this dangerous?" I asked.

"Yes," he said. "You probably shouldn't walk this way alone."

Between Bernice Court and the subway, we passed three laundromats—one decorated like a circus—two Chinese takeout places and a restaurant called Fried Chicken and Pizza, which had a red plastic awning and, in a gesture of pluralism, also served "bagel/roll with butter." There were several beauty salons, all evidently named during an era when putting a *z* in words made them look cooler: Appearancez was one, Hair Stylz another. On the corner of Troy and Eastern Parkway was a liquor store called Liquor Store. A few men hung around outside, drinking from bottles concealed in brown paper bags. During our walk, Cosmo told me about his love of psychedelic punk rock and then tried to explain to me what psyche-delic punk rock was.

"Bye," he said when we got to the subway, then turned on his heels and left.

I rode the subway back to Manhattan to meet friends for fajitas on the Upper West Side. The one thought in my head as the train chugged uptown was, "Thank God I'll never see *that* guy again."

THE NEXT DAY, in search of some fatherly advice, I went to visit one of the treasured adults in my life, a man who runs a television network, whom I'd met years earlier as a reporter for the *Observer*. As always, Richard was warm and kind. He gave me a hug and, in a tender show of concern, asked his secretary to hold his calls. We went into his vast corner office, full of pictures of his wife and daughter, and I trained my gaze on the ribbed fabric of his couch. This was one of the people in the city I'd always referred to as my "rabbis." Wise and well connected, he tended to give good advice and seemed to take pleasure in doing so.

"All men under the age of forty are just walking boners," he said after I told him what had happened with Chad. "Don't take it personally." He promised it would all work out.

The next day, I went to visit my old boss, the eccentric former editor of the *New York Observer*. Peter always wore the same frayed khaki trousers and crumpled blue shirts, with his tie tucked in, like Napoleon's hand, between the third and fourth button. He always seemed more made up than real to me, an impression enhanced by the virtual impossibility of seeing him. Wise, reclusive and perpetually harried, he is one of the very few people I've met who could make any young writer feel worthwhile.

"Rebecca, I have three things to tell you," he said, sliding a chocolate chip cookie across the table and under my nose. "First, you need to gain fifteen pounds immediately. Don't do the anorexia thing right now, will you? It's boring."

I broke off a tiny piece and took a bite. The cookie was soft, buttery and a little warm, and I felt a drop of chocolate melt in the middle of my tongue. On any other day, this would have been a positive experience, but on that day, it felt garish and obscene, as if my senses were under attack. I swallowed and smiled painfully.

He continued. "Second, what's your natural hair color?" I gestured at my eyebrows, which were my natural plain brown, where the pixie-cut mop on my head was an otherworldly shade called platinum ice. "Go back to it," he said.

Third was a recommendation to "throw yourself into your work." I finished off the cookie even though it felt like battery acid on my throat.

"How old are you?" he asked.

"Twenty-seven."

"Good," he said. "You have one year left."

He didn't say for what, and I was too afraid to ask.

"Do you have a good therapist?" he said.

"Yes," I said.

"Good," he said. "Get her to cut you a special rate and go in twice or three times a week through New Year's."

"Okay," I said, having no intention of bargaining with my therapist.

"Where are you living?" he said.

"On a friend's couch." He looked at me disapprovingly.

"I went yesterday to see this horrible apartment in the middle of Crown Heights. It was disgusting, and I think the guy who lives there is a Hasid," I said. He pressed, and I told him a few more details: it was big and open, I'd have my own room, the neighborhood was horrible, like a scene out of *A Stranger Among Us*. It was cheap, and it was the last place I could ever imagine myself.

Peter thought for a moment.

"You should do it," he said.

After their lives implode, some people stay put and settle into the hole where everything used to be. This is what Chad did, as far as I know: just stuck it out in the apartment, staring at the spot where my television once sat. Other people, faced with the void, do something dramatic. They go to Mexico for a week or Argentina for a year or a convent for the rest of their lives. Given endless means, I would have run away too. But, as unglamorous as it was, I had to support myself. When you're alone in the world, you don't just drop everything and run off to India to meditate twenty hours a day and assume you'll be able to get another job at some point, especially not one with free soy lattes and Friday brunch. Given these restrictions, about the farthest I could run was the place at the very end of the subway line.

The next morning I sent Cosmo an e-mail saying I'd like to take the room. The reply came back immediately.

hi!
likewise.

TWO DAYS LATER, I brought him the deposit and first month's rent, $975, in cash. Lubavitchers commonly don't accept checks.

Mars for a Price

On November 15, my two best friends from college, Annie and Matthew, came with me to my old apartment to help me pack and move. I went expecting postearthquake devastation. I went expecting to spend hours weeping over the desecration of my home. I brought thirty-five dollars' worth of fancy pastries, which I thought we'd slowly work through, as I held up mementos from my one great love, sobbing, telling the story of how we came to acquire such and such thing and what sentimental value it carried. I burned Lady Gaga's "Bad Romance" onto a CD and planned to play it on repeat the entire time.

Ra ra, raaaahh ahhh ahhh
Romah, romah mahhh

That morning I'd prepared for the move with a trip to Bed Bath & Beyond, where I selected one blanket, one pillow, one set of sheets, one roll of packing tape and one bath towel, then fainted on the way to checkout. It was a terrible mess at the time, but there are worse places to lose consciousness than a giant home-supply store. Immediately, three blue-aproned employees descended, wielding Kleenex tissue pocket packs, sanitary hand wipes and bottles of Poland Spring. I was mortified and, for as long as the embarrassment lasted, relieved.

It was another obnoxiously beautiful day. When we arrived at 82 Jane Street, I walked around in a daze, waiting for the first reminder of all I'd lost to set me bawling. But it never happened. Here, in a drawer, were the twelve new pairs of black dress socks I'd bought him the other week. There, in the closet, was the gray scarf we traded back and forth. In the freezer was a half-empty bottle of fancy vodka I'd given him as a present when he left the law firm. We'd had good times, and there were reminders of those, but there was no evidence of the fairy-tale romance I was sure I'd lost. There was nothing in all our shared six hundred square feet that catapulted me into a sorrow-tinged reverie about "that time when"—when he really saw me, when we really connected. Had those times ever happened? They must have, but the evidence didn't bear it out.

It took an hour and a half to pack everything. We worked in silence. Matthew, recently engaged to his boyfriend Ted, boxed books. Annie, recently engaged to her boyfriend Santosh, handled clothing and toiletries. I have always been inept at packing, and with the added obstacles of sleep deprivation and grief, I mostly wandered around, dropping items in boxes

where they didn't belong, leaving Annie, meticulous and effi-
cient, to trail me, fixing everything. Nothing on the walls was
mine. There were no mutual possessions in dispute, except
the scarf, which I took. I had sold off all my furniture, donated
my pillows, sheets, towels, pots, pans and silverware when
we'd moved in together. When I moved out, the hardest part
was seeing how few typical grown-up-person things I actually
owned. There was a lamp, an ottoman, an area rug, a television, six boxes of books, three of clothing and shoes, and one
of miscellany. My entire earthly footprint: enough to fill a
shopping cart.

Before the movers came, we laid out the few items I'd cap-
tured in my trawling that seemed to carry some real emotional
heft. There was a hand-drawn card from our second anniversary. There was a sheet with three photo-booth pictures from
a friend's wedding, showing us making two silly faces and
then me kissing him on the cheek. There were assorted cards
and letters from his parents, sent to me on Jewish holidays.
And there was a stuffed toy Eeyore he'd brought me a year
earlier, when he picked me up from having my wisdom teeth
removed.

Of these, only Eeyore was perilous. When you squeezed a
button sewn into the toy donkey's hoof, a speaker buried in
his belly emitted a low, melancholy version of "Blue Christmas," a holiday song about unrequited love that was made
famous by Elvis Presley and later covered by the Beach Boys. It
had seemed like a strange postsurgery gift when I got it, but
I'd had the operation six days before Thanksgiving, and that's

what was on offer at the drugstore across the street, where Chad went before picking me up. I'd been terrified about the surgery for weeks before it happened, fears driven by a full mental catalog of bad hospital experiences from my youth. I was not exactly hearty as a child. I was by far the smallest girl in my school—short, rail thin, nicknamed Shrimpy Wimpy by a six-year-old tyrant who would grow to be only five foot one, a full nine inches shorter than my adult height. I had an undiagnosed blood disorder that stripped me of energy and kept my immune system, as a defense force, on par with the Iraqi national guard. (This condition was later diagnosed, incorrectly, by the Yale University Department of Undergraduate Health—nicknamed Duh—as sickle cell anemia. I did an actual spit-take when the poor nurse came in to break the news. I am not only the palest but also in every sense the *whitest* girl who ever lived. The condition was later correctly diagnosed as alpha thalassemia, which basically means "really tiny red blood cells," and which is like having an untreatable case of anemia. You're a little schleppy all the time, and there's nothing you can do about it. It will shock no one to learn that this is a genetic disorder that turns up in Jews.)

In addition to being weak, anemic, underweight and really into math, I was also violently allergic to every known antibiotic. This was my lot, and I accepted it. While every other kid at school got to guzzle bubble-gum-flavored penicillin any time she had strep throat, I spent a few weeks in and out of the hospital, hooked up to a heart monitor, taking teeny tiny doses of medicine intravenously. I lay in the hospital bed, in my hospital gown and my hospital socks, and stared up at the drip, drip, drip of the IV machine, wondering if this was the drip that was going to send me into shock (again) and maybe, probably, finish me off. These visits, which happened once a year or so, were the only times in my life I have ever prayed without any prompting or company. I didn't know how to do it, so I copied the nursery rhyme. When no one was looking, I put my hands together, palm to palm ("Here is the church, here is the steeple . . ."), and spoke my message straight to God: "I'm sorry I only talk to you when I need something," I'd whisper. "People probably don't ask often, so how are you? I hope you're doing well." (It's not that I was interested, really, but I was a precocious suck-up.) "Listen, can you just not kill me yet?"

No medical procedure in my life had ever worked out as planned, and so, going into the wisdom tooth extraction I'd put off for a decade, I was feeling fatalistic—justifiably so, it turned out. Complications from the surgery sent me to the hospital for three days, in physical pain not even an IV cocktail of morphine and Dilaudid could touch. I developed an abscess that effectively locked my lower jaw shut. On the plus side, I spoke like a country club WASP, which was funny for a while. On the minus, the swelling began to choke off my airway. Three times a day, two oral surgeons came to my hospital room to check on whatever evil had taken residence in my skull. To do so, they executed a medieval procedure that involved jimmying my jaw open with a wooden tongue depressor. Chad held my toes and whispered that everything was going to be okay. He never once left my bedside. I was blitzed on painkillers, disoriented and terrified. The doctors decided I needed emergency surgery. "I'm afraid I'm not going to wake up," I told Chad through my clenched jaw. He stroked my hair. I held Eeyore so tight that after three days the stuffing around his chest cavity had large dents in the shape of my fist.

"What do you want to do with this?" Annie asked, dangling the donkey by one leg.

I formed my hand around Eeyore's belly and felt a lump rising in my throat. Annie left me alone with my stuffed animal, scuttling off to the bedroom for one final sweep. A large white Hefty bag lay open in front of me, full of newspapers, half-used bottles of shampoo, nail polish remover and empty rolls of packing tape. I've never been a person who holds on to things. I didn't have a camera, didn't keep ticket stubs or old friendship bracelets. Where would I put this if I did take it with me? In a drawer somewhere, so I'd happen on it many years later and be transported back to a painful episode that the first love of my life helped me survive, sometime after he started harping about my posture and before he started cheating on me? I looked into Eeyore's droopy plastic eyes and reconsidered. Any memento of goodness, however isolated, must be worth holding on to, I thought. Even if it's nothing more than a reminder that there wasn't only badness. Right?

Annie marched back from her sweep of the bedroom, holding something small in her hand that I couldn't quite make out.

"Do you want to keep this hair thing?" she asked. "You left it on your night table."

My hair was cropped short. I didn't use or own hair things, let alone leave them on my night table, which was plainly no longer my night table. One of my hands, the one not holding Eeyore, drifted up to my head. Annie's face fell. She put the plastic clip down on what was no longer my kitchen table. I could see now that a few long brown hairs were tangled in its teeth.

Annie was a resident at the hospital where I went after my jaw locked shut, and she also sat next to my bed there. She was with me when the doctors said I needed surgery, and when I said I was afraid I'd never wake up, she said, "Everyone's afraid of that, and it just doesn't happen." Then, with all the love in her heart, she said, "Don't be an idiot, Rebecca. You're going to be fine." And I was fine. No surgery. Sometime in the middle of the third night, as they were prepping a bed, the abscess just disappeared. Like it had never been there.

I stared at the hair clip on the table. My gaze drifted over to the Particularity Qatar! shirt, with the three stick-figure donkeys, balled up in the corner of the couch, and I reflected for a minute on how the enduring image of the last three years of my life was that of an ass. Annie came over, took the Eeyore toy out of my hand and threw it in the garbage.

The doll landed on its leg and started to sing. "I'll have a *blooooooooo* Christmas without *yoooo*. I'll be so *blooooooooooo* just thinking about *yoooo*."

Annie walked over to the garbage bag and with one

sneakered foot stomped on Eeyore until we heard a plastic snap, then a few metallic burbles and then, finally, silence.

"OH," SAID COSMO, returning home from work later after I'd moved in. "You're here, I see."

I smiled weakly.

"And you've been talking to the boyfriend?"

I'd spoken to the boyfriend, and then I'd spent the better part of the afternoon sobbing into my brand-new Sealy Posture Premier mattress. The giveaway here was my giant red face.

Mhmmm. Cosmo nodded. He stroked his beard, taking an almost physical pleasure in the affirmation of his suspicions, in the unfailing predictability of women. "I am very smart, you know," he said and pushed past me toward the kitchen to put a kettle on, flipping the light switch on the way.

I followed him on tiptoe, as if the less I touched the ground, the less real any of this would be. The kitchen was, let's say, spartan. A plastic table and two red plastic chairs occupied one wall. A few stray pots and pans sat by the sink. The Frigidaire was basically empty, emitted a distinctly toxic smell and hadn't been cleaned in so long—possibly ever—that a rainbow of early-stage antibiotic cultures covered the interior walls. The floor was sticky, grabbing the pads of my feet, discouraging movement. I hovered in the doorframe.

"We should give you something real to drink," Cosmo said, stretching up and pulling a giant box of Sho Chiku Bai sake from the shelf. I stared at his array of magnets advertising kosher pizza shops and delivery meat markets. A small, painted-ceramic klezmer band played a tiny Celsius thermometer like an instrument on his freezer door. He slid the bottle out of the box and sloshed around the contents: a few tablespoons of foamy liquid a little too thick to be palatable booze. "It's old but I think still good?"

I shook my head and sniffled. "Just tea, thanks."

My cheeks were inflated like a party balloon, my internal organs twisted into a hot coil, my sinuses on the verge of collapse. Cosmo rolled a cigarette. He sat down and smoked it slowly and indulgently. When the kettle started screaming, he let it scream, finishing his cigarette and flicking ashes in the big metal sink.

"I have a date this week," I said. Something benign and nonthreatening, hastily arranged by a colleague.

"You will probably sabotage it," he replied, poking at the end of his perfectly rolled cigarette with one blunt fingertip, the nail clipped short and clean.

We drank our tea sitting opposite each other at the kitchen table, which was covered in plastic bags from House of Glatt and a box of six-month-old handmade Israeli matzos. This was November, Passover was in the spring.

"Why don't you get rid of these?" I asked.

"They're expensive," he said.

Cosmo prepared another cigarette. Watching felt like voyeurism, not least because before I moved in, he had typically done these things alone, and most private indulgences, no matter how benign, take on a sensual quality. He pinched a

too-fat wad of tobacco and let it fall loosely onto the rolling
paper, which he twisted between his fingers until it was a perfect tube. He licked one edge, careful not to extend his tongue
beyond his lips, hypercognizant, like all ultrareligious people,
of the exposure of body parts to open air. I watched, pushing
up the sleeve on my T-shirt so it rested on top of my
shoulder—a mindless habit. In all my years of heathen living,
of promiscuity and impiety and the mixing of milk and meat,
I had never seen someone roll a cigarette so intently. It wasn't
until much later that I realized he'd rarely been that close to a
woman's bare arm before.

"Do you know of this book, *Exodus*?" he asked, looking
down.

"Like, from the Bible?" I said, trying to smile politely.

"No!" He looked disgusted. "The one about the boat."

After an extended back and forth that touched on Exodus,
the band, I learned he meant the book by Leon Uris about
a ship full of Jews that fled a detention camp in Cyprus in
1947 and sailed for what was then Palestine. It is the story of
the founding of the Jewish state. It became a movie, directed
by Otto Preminger, starring Paul Newman.

"Oh," I said finally. "The Paul Newman one."

Cosmo looked at me with exhaustion and nodded once for
"Yes, moron."

"The author of this book, which I have not read, wrote
a story, which I did read." He was leaning against the sink
now, his forearms resting on his chenille yarmulke, which was
held on by a single bobby pin. ("Bobby pins are the begin-

ning," he would tell me later. The beginning of what? "Of vanity. For a Lubavitcher, it all goes downhill from there.") This
was a favorite pose of his, vaguely rabbinical but also poetic,
allowing him a wide berth to gesture dramatically, jabbing his
cigarette in the air. "The story is about a man who is married
for a long time and then gets divorced, and the point of it is
that it's a natural state for a writer to be lonely and sad." He
seemed genuinely pleased by this parable, as if it were the
answer to all my distress. "You know, Rebecca, you may be
alone for a very long time."

I thanked him for the insight by staggering off to our shared
bathroom with the intention of vomiting in the little toilet
with the blue opalescent clam-shaped plastic top. My stomach
had been doing this a lot lately, sending me spinning off to
bathrooms, where I'd curl up on the cold tiles next to the toilet
and pray for some outward expression of the internal collapse
I felt. It never came.

I sat on the edge of the bathtub and looked up fourteen
feet to the water-stained ceiling, with its single lightbulb and
unreachable pull chain. On the windowsill, there was a three-
year-old copy of *Spin* magazine and a book of sheet music.
The tiny gray floor tiles were caked with brown grime, as was
the sink basin and the bottom edge of the shower curtain,
dangling by too few hooks from a pencil-thin metal rod.
When was the last time a woman had been in this room?
Never, I guessed. Three toothbrushes, a box of Q-tips and a
bright red canister of Axe deodorant body spray occupied the
only shelves.

I noticed a yellowed piece of paper hanging on the wall just outside the door and stumbled over to take a look. It had a series of short Hebrew prayers followed by English translations. The last and longest was:

You are blessed, Lord our God, sovereign of the world, who formed man cleverly, and created in him many different organs and channels. It is clearly evident before Your glorious throne that, should one of these be wrongly opened, or one of them be wrongly blocked, it would be impossible to continue to stand before You. You are blessed, Lord, who heals all flesh in a wonderful way.

This prayer hung six feet from my new toilet, which had horrible plumbing, in my new apartment, which, while only five miles or thirty minutes by subway from my old home, was an infinite distance in space and time from my old life. For a second I imagined what I would be doing if I were still on planet Earth, as I once knew it. I would be curled up on the couch, eating takeout sushi and watching premium cable with the man of my obliterated dreams.

"How the hell did I get here?" I thought, meaning both existentially and literally. How did my perfect life come to this? And also, How, physically, did I end up curled around some ultra-Orthodox rabbi's glorious throne in the middle of Brooklyn? It had all been such a blur.

"Rebecca!" Cosmo called. "Dinnertime!"

I hadn't eaten in days. My many organs and channels

were processing vodka, Valium and the trauma of a failed relationship—little else. "Come on already!" Cosmo said. "We go shopping!"

Crown Heights is home to the world's largest community of Lubavitch-Hasidim, a sect of ultra-Orthodox Jews with a New Age bent, estimated to be about two hundred thousand strong and growing. They live much the same way their fathers, grandfathers and great-grandfathers lived in territories more hostile than remote Brooklyn, where Jews were driven out by angry mobs on good days, murdered and tossed into mass graves on bad ones. The men, known colloquially as "black hats," wear black hats, black coats, long beards and prayer shawls. The women wear long dresses or skirts and tops that cover knees and elbows. The rabbis commonly look like the face cards from my Memory Game: old, grizzled and gray. The children, of whom there are seemingly infinite numbers, are adorable.

One thing that sets Lubavitchers apart from more mainstream Jews—the regular Orthodox, the Conservative, the Reform, and the godless heathens like me—is that they're driven by a belief in the Messiah's imminent return. Because of this, they recruit like the army in wartime, sending out fleets of mitzvah tanks—painted buses that roll around the city spreading the word of God—and setting up Chabad Houses around the world. They train their smartest sons, like Cosmo, to become rabbis, then ship them off to distant lands to teach Jews to be more observant and non-Jews to do the best they can, poor fools. A year before I moved to Crown

Heights, Muslim terrorists from Pakistan bombed ten separate sites in Mumbai, India, one of which was a Chabad House run by Rabbi Gabi Holtzberg and his wife, Rivka, a young couple killed in the attack. This kind of warfare is devastating but not surprising to the descendants of the original Lubavitchers, whose parents and grandparents schlepped to America from Lyubavichi, in what is now Russia, while the Russians and the Germans and pretty much everyone else on the planet ran after them with torches. This is a community that has fully internalized the magnitude of its struggle, embracing its urgency and its dire consequence. They have, as the Mafia would say, gone to the mattresses for the Jewish soul.

And I had come to them, and gone to my own mattress, and sobbed.

"The answer is that crying cannot rebuild," Menachem Mendel Schneerson wrote in volume ten of a particularly sexy work called *Likkutei Sichot*, an underappreciated reference for young atheists in the throes of their first heartbreaks. Schneerson was the beating heart of the Lubavitch community, a man with small eyes and a thick beard who captivated his followers. His teachings were so vibrantly apocalyptic and he was such a compelling, enigmatic figure that many, including Cosmo, started to think Schneerson himself was the Messiah. When he died in 1994 and the world didn't end, the Lubavitchers went about rebuilding. Among the gifts Schneerson passed on to his tribe, which aided them in this task, was a prodigious talent for fund-raising. Coffers brimming, they have continued to spread the word in their leader's absence, performing mitzvoth, or good deeds, as he, and God before him, commanded.

Don't be a pansy, the teaching goes, *do something*. In a year after the Mumbai bombing, Lubavitchers the world over raised enough money to carry little Moisheleh, the Holtzberg's orphaned two-year-old son, to adulthood, and, *mertz Hashem*, God willing, through rabbinical school. "Crying lessens the pain," Schneerson wrote in *Likkutei Sichot*, "but it cannot fix what was destroyed."

Well, if crying wasn't going to do it, what then?

"Rebecca!" Cosmo's calls grew louder from the kitchen. "It's time to eat!"

For as much outreach as they do in the world, the Crown Heights Lubavitchers like to come home to their own. They have formed an airtight community in the middle of the most populous county in New York. Street signs are written in Yiddish. Proper decorum is enforced by a crew of rabbis and other sticklers known locally as the "*tsnius* police." (*Tsnius* is the Yiddish word for traditional conservative dress, and those who police it go to great lengths to make sure Hasids aren't bombarded by sexy female elbows and knees.) Duck underground for thirty minutes and you emerge from the subway into the cheating heart of the modern world. You can watch a drag queen sodomize himself with a wine bottle on the stage of a popular nightclub or do blow off the anatomy of a male model in the bathroom of a penthouse or sit uncomfortably close to an eminent journalist during a dinner party in an Upper East Side town house, and try not to look as he runs his fingers up the skirt of a senior member of the Council on Foreign Relations. Back down in the subway, and half an hour later, the year appears to be 1702.

Some younger Lubavitchers refer to their neighborhood as just the "'chood," pronounced with a soft "k" at the back of the throat, the universal consonant of Jews. The 'chood is bordered on all sides by black neighborhoods, composed largely of West Indian immigrants. Long before the 1991 Crown Heights riots that left three dead and the neighborhood devastated, the different communities of central Brooklyn were at war, over not only this world but also the next. Cosmo and I lived right on the edge of the West Indian neighborhood, and unlike my old apartment in the West Village, inhabited exclusively by white upper-middle-class yuppies and right down the street from where they filmed *Sex and the City*, my new apartment building was half blacks, half Jews. "The blacks are nicer," Cosmo said as we walked through the building and the silent battle of opposing apocalypses that played out on our neighbors' doors. TIME IS SHORT. JESUS IS COMING! said the bumper sticker on C6. MOSHIACH IS COMING! LET'S GET READY! proclaimed B3. Someone in D4 had typed up a Malcolm X quote and taped it to his door:

I believe in the brotherhood of man, all men, but I don't believe in brotherhood with anybody who doesn't want brotherhood with me. I believe in treating people right, but I'm not going to waste my time trying to treat somebody right who doesn't know how to return the treatment.

The central courtyard, paved over in cement, hosted a strange collection of discarded items that never budged as long as I lived there: a broken child's car seat, several windows, half an old station wagon divided into its component parts. Everything about the place seemed to suggest it was the last stop at the end of the world.

As we walked to a corner store in the West Indian neighborhood, me sniffling into a balled-up tissue, Cosmo breathing in the night air, we passed pairs of women pushing giant multiple-baby strollers and groups of young Hasidic men straining against the wind. Everyone stared at us.

"Is everyone staring at us?" I asked.

"Yes."

"Is that because you're not supposed to be walking down the street with me?"

"Yes."

"Is that because I look like a shiksa?" (This is a derogatory Yiddish term for a non-Jewish woman.)

"It's because you look like a German."

We walked a way in silence.

"I think I'm going to dye my hair," I said.

"Do I at least get a say in the color?"

"No."

"You should dye it blue."

Silence.

"Why did you let me take the room, if this is all so forbidden?" I asked.

"Why not?" he said, affectless.

"You're rebelling, or something, is that it?"

"Whatever."

It took a long time to piece together the details of Cosmo's past because he prefers dramatic gestures and untranslatable expressions to traditional linear storytelling. It also took a long time because he is an evasive, cagey, complicated and lonely person who had never really been interrogated about his life story before. Like me, he had what polite people would call a healthy imagination. In his view, he worked at a copy shop but belonged on a battlefield. "Is there a place that needs to have a revolution? I really believe that's my calling," he said once. "I'm Trotsky. I'm Jabotinsky. I should be leading armies through Prussia. I shouldn't be . . . here."

That first night in Crown Heights, I taught Cosmo how to cook spaghetti, and it was the first time I stopped crying for more than an hour in days. It's not that he didn't know, per se, but he'd always cooked the noodles for at least twenty-five minutes, to make sure they were good and soft. I introduced him to the concept of al dente. "Is it!" he said. This was his all-purpose exclamation for things that surprised him.

I watched him eat dinner but couldn't eat any myself.

"Do you like chocolate?" he asked.

I nodded.

"We'll have to get some and melt it on the stove and inject it into your veins."

"Sounds delicious," I said.

Cosmo told me he liked a full-bodied woman. His favorite actress was Kate Winslet. (His favorite actor was Brad Pitt, whom he believed—not entirely without merit—was his perfect doppelgänger). He worshipped Lars von Trier. He was curious about my life but also unaccustomed to the porous boundaries of the Western world and cautious about asking too many questions. He wanted to be friends on Facebook. He wanted to come out dancing with my friends sometime.

"Will it be like *Sex and the City*?" he asked.

"Yes and no," I said.

Lost Messiah

I didn't learn Cosmo was a rabbi until after I moved in, when he breezily announced that I should do whatever I wanted with the living room furniture except I should speak to him if I was going to throw away the bookcase, because hidden somewhere in it was his rabbinical certificate. I took the news in stride. The bookcase was the least of the living room's problems, a much lower priority than the mauve-colored faux leather couch with the giant gash in the middle and stuffing tufting out, or the twelve-foot-long oval oak dining table that occupied a full two-thirds of the room. Also, it was difficult to get too excited about furniture when I was pretty sure I wouldn't survive the winter.

The initial burst of clarity that sent me to Crown Heights quickly gave way to bottomless self-pity and a general lack of interest in life. I basically stopped eating, since all food tasted too strong. I walked around wearing headphones with no music playing, since street sounds felt like someone was jack-hammering a hole into my head. I wore sunglasses because even though sweet death seemed imminent, I was still terri-fied of getting wrinkles. So, not everything changed. *You have one year left.*

Cosmo and I confounded each other at the beginning. Typ-ically, you meet a new person and have at least a basic sense of the social rules governing the interaction. "Oh, hi" (hand-shake), "I'm Rebecca" (eye contact), "nice to meet you." And in under ten words, there is now a shared humanity. I'm taller, you're shorter. I'm dressed up, you're dressed down. Look how much time I clearly spend on my hair! I'm probably a narcissist, but also I have an easy smile and a big laugh, so I'm almost certainly not *Satan.* You make a thousand instantaneous judg-ments in the first moments of meeting someone, and mostly they're correct.

I had no such experience with Cosmo. The semiotics were completely out of whack. He could have been a learned scholar, an unemployed hipster or a roadie for Ozzfest. His hair was rust colored, cropped close on the pate with a thick beard about half a foot long at its tip. He wore T-shirts and slacks over a pair of brown men's dress shoes so dilapidated they looked like they might disappear in a cloud of dust. When he smiled, it stretched out and sprang back like a rub-ber band, giving no indication of pleasure or displeasure, friendliness or disinterest or sarcasm. It worked like a comma in his speech. "Do whatever you want with the living room furniture" (quick smile) "but speak to me before you do anything with the bookcase, because hidden somewhere in there is my rabbinical certificate."

"Wait," I said, "you're a rabbi?"

"Yes" (quick smile), "although the older I get, the less I think I qualify."

"But you work at a photocopy shop?"

"Yes."

"Do you like it?"

"No."

"Why don't you leave?"

"Because" (quick smile) "I'm waiting for my papers to come through."

"How long have you been waiting?"

"Seven years."

Quick smile.

I tried to be polite, but who knows what polite is under such circumstances, when the proper thing to do was to never have been there in the first place. In the absence of a better idea, I smiled back obsequiously. I did a lot of obsequious smiling in those first days, when I wasn't sobbing or sulking around, and the result was we looked something like Annie's old ward at Bellevue. One person grinning like an idiot, the other flashing glimpses of his teeth—friendly or unfriendly, it wasn't clear.

THE MORNING AFTER I moved in, I woke up in the apartment, my eyes puffy and red. I stumbled to the kitchen to get a glass of water and found Cosmo standing at the stove, in underwear and *tzitzit*, frying eggs. "What's up?" he said, slightly annoyed, as if I were interrupting.

As far as I knew, Cosmo had never lived with a woman before, and after I moved in, he didn't change much. He sang whenever it moved him, belting Hebrew raps and Paul Simon ballads with the full capacity of his lungs. He had an unparalleled tolerance for grating noise. He was impervious to screaming teakettles and to his alarm clock in the morning, which began beeping slowly and sped up until it sounded like a person flatlining on an EKG machine. He'd let it go for hours. (For the first few weeks I lived there, I woke every morning with an acute sensation of having just been pronounced dead.)

"With jujitsu, I estimate I'll be able to take out a group of five to seven black men," Cosmo told me that morning as he ate his eggs. "Oh, I forgot to mention, there was a robbing at gunpoint right outside our lobby last week. A man from the apartment chased the guy down, and it turned out to be a real gun! Not loaded, though." A note of genuine disappointment rang in his voice.

In his atheist manifesto *God Is Not Great*, in a chapter called "Religion Kills," Christopher Hitchens relates a hypothetical question, posed to him by religious broadcaster Dennis Prager when the two sat together on a panel, which Hitchens locates in time "a week before the events of September 11, 2001." The question was: If you were walking through a strange city in the evening and saw a large group of men approaching, would you feel more or less safe if you knew they were just coming from a prayer meeting? Hitchens's answer is "less safe" in the extreme, and he recounts six illustrative personal experiences that occurred only within the letter *B*—Belfast, Beirut, Bombay, Belgrade, Bethlehem and Baghdad—to which I, never having been to those places but agreeing wholeheartedly with the sentiment, would only add: Brooklyn.

It wasn't just the Jews, it was everyone. When I walked alone from the subway on my way home from work at ten, eleven, twelve o'clock at night, I felt comfortably certain that everyone on the street was just about to rape or murder me. I had been taught this since grade school, when the principal brought in a special speaker to address my fifth-grade class about how to fend off the sexual assault that no doubt loomed in our future. She was a short, angry woman with a gym teacher's build. I remember two key pieces of advice: "Always wear sneakers or shoes you can sprint in." Sprinting was essential. And: "Carry a whistle." I did neither of these things, especially not the former. I am five foot ten, and I have no earthly need to wear high heels—and in fact many incentives not to wear them—but unless I was going running or to the beach, I never left home in anything else. This was a point of pride, and it became an inviolable tenet once I moved to Crown Heights. Since whistles weren't an option either—mostly because *who carries a whistle?*—I developed a different mechanism for feeling safe when I walked home alone at night. I sang.

To say I am not a singer is an understatement on par with "I am not an ultra-Orthodox Jew." I played piano growing up, studying the Suzuki method with the mild-mannered Mrs. Kaufman, whom my father called "the cough woman" and who was so fragile she seemed to have been glued together like pieces of a broken vase. Then came more rigorous classical instruction with a Russian woman, who banged the wall to keep tempo as I played, and ultimately broke up with me via handwritten note to my parents. Her name was Snitkovsky.

If I had one wish, I would wish for the ability to sing. I tried to teach myself once as a kid: in the public library, with a book called *Teach Yourself to Sing!* It didn't work. We were forced to take singing class at Ellis, but I was so embarrassed by my weak, warbly voice I cried every time I was forced to solo. Being generally nerdy and unaccustomed to struggling at school, I reacted to this by acting out, finding ever new and barbaric ways of tormenting our teacher, Mrs. Crosby, a kind enough woman with terrible nerves. Mrs. Crosby cried when my fellow atonal brats and I did nasty things, like humming while she spoke, one at a time, switching just as she laid eyes on us, so she could never locate the source of the noise. Entire classes were wasted like this, and entire afternoons spent in the principal's office. In high school, to satisfy our music requirement, I played poorly in a jazz band. This was the whole of my experience with musical performance until I became a resident lunatic in the 'chood.

What I lack in musical ability, I at least make up for with enthusiasm. It's possible that no one is more susceptible than I am to the emotional pull of pop music. I was the only kid with a Walkman on my bus in elementary school, and I played Michael Jackson as loud as the volume dial went. One year for Hanukkah, I requested and got a white Pocket Rocker handheld minicassette player and listened to "Walk Like an Egyptian" until the tape wore out. There is almost nothing I don't like, and in many cases, the worse the better: I lived for Ace of Base, Boyz II Men, Kris Kross, Green Day, every terrible Europop invasion and every teen-slut nightmare built from plastic in Orlando. For my fourteenth birthday, I took two friends to see Ani DiFranco at a tiny club in downtown Pittsburgh and found the whole experience so transcendent—all the short-haired women bouncing around, armpit fur blowing in the air-conditioning—I spent two weeks convinced I was a lesbian. I have seen Phish and the Dave Matthews Band at least a dozen times. I have spent hours sobbing to Fleetwood Mac and Alanis Morissette. When I graduated to a Discman, the first disc I bought was a compilation of pop hits from 1983.

The first night I came home to Crown Heights, I tucked my iPod into my handbag for the walk home—all the better to hear my attacker as he crept up behind me, ether-soaked rag in hand. Once I did this, every sound immediately seemed threatening. Every person, by extension, seemed even more like a predator. I had moved to a neighborhood where, if you looked out through squinting eyes, everyone appeared to be a comic book villain. The Jews were all cloaked in black. There was a less than wholesome crowd perpetually lingering outside Liquor Store, and down the street was a dog kennel, whose employees always seemed to choose odd hours for loading and unloading crates of pit bulls from a dented white van. That first night, I had made it halfway home, my heart pounding in my ears, my fingers pinched together (all the better to jam into the eyeballs of an attacker, per the security expert), when my calm gave out. I sprinted the rest of the way home, in nonapproved ultra-high heels.

The next night was a modest improvement—I made it one more block before running—and on night three, I tried a different tack. I kept my headphones on. Jay-Z was playing when I left the subway, and Jay-Z walked me home. Midway, the loud barking of a pit bull interrupted the trance of Hova, and I jumped in fear. But instead of sprinting, I started rapping along.

She got an ass that'll swallow up a g-string
And up top, uh, two bee stings

I rapped these verses like I was trying to scare away bears in the forest. I rapped them like a white girl with less than no chance of having sickle cell anemia. I did this every night from then on, and somehow, no doubt in spite of my fresh beats, not because of them, I managed not to be killed.

Mornings were generally better, but not by much. One

lovely Wednesday shortly after I moved in, around nine a.m., I was walking to the subway with my headphones in, music blaring, dressed in what for me was pretty traditional work wear: knee-high boots, leather leggings, a short black shift that fell somewhere around my upper thigh, with a prim little green plaid button-up shirt underneath and a simple blazer on top. This was one of my favorite outfits. It emphasized my height and gave me the sort of confidence only a favorite outfit can give—that last-ditch feeling of presence in the world, when the one thing keeping you upright is your clothes. The music in my headphones was loud but not loud enough to entirely drown out a guttural scream from across the street. It couldn't possibly be directed at me, I figured, so I kept walking. But the scream grew louder. I took out one earbud.

"Where's your dress!"

That's what it sounded like at least. I scanned the sidewalk. Crown Street had a gentle dusting of fall leaves. The sky was bright blue and the air was clear. It was a brisk, lovely fall day. The brownstones that lined the street were stately, and if you didn't look closely at all the signs warning of Moshiach's imminent return, this could have been the set of *The Cosby Show*. It was an idyllic New York morning.

My eyes ran along the horizon until I saw him—a tiny furious member of the *tsnius* police, maybe five foot four. He had a long salt-and-pepper beard, wore a black hat and black coat and jabbed an index finger high into the perfect fall air.

"Where's your dress! Where's your dress!"

I looked down at my legs. My "dress," such as it was, was peeping out maybe a half inch beneath the bottom seam of my blazer. It was demonstrably there, right on my body, but somehow I didn't think that kind of logic would prevail.

I kept walking. He kept screaming. It was four blocks to the subway, and he shouted the whole time. If I hadn't already felt like a charred nub of former life, I would have curled up and died. The entire neighborhood—all the mothers out on the streets, all the little boys scuttling off to yeshiva, all the men buying donuts at the kosher grocery store on Kingston Avenue—turned and stared at me. I could sing at night to fend off the rapists, but I found myself powerless in the face of sheer scorn.

First came the wave of indignation. Who do these people think they are? This is America! I'm a woman! I'm free and independent, and what's more, this dress is Diane von Furstenberg—*hello?*

"Where's your dress!"

I took it as established fact that every female member of the Crown Heights Lubavitch community was horribly oppressed and every male was not only an oppressor but also a lout. I'd collected my Susan B. Anthony coins as a proper Ellis girl. I'd read my Steinem. Hell, I once tracked down Shulamith Firestone, the radical feminist who advocated a "smile boycott" on the theory that even a woman's most basic expression of pleasure had been co-opted into merely a device for flirtation, designed to titillate men. (She lived in a brownstone on East

11th Street, and she didn't answer the doorbell when I rang, with hopes of interviewing her about Sarah Palin.) The point here is that I considered myself a feminist. I was the daughter of a feminist. My teachers had been feminists, and my peers, male and female, were feminists as well. If there was one thing I could recognize, it was oppression.

"Where's your dress!"

I saw oppression without even looking, really—since I was afraid to make eye contact—in the frumpy dresses and crooked wigs of the women of Crown Heights. In the way they walked around pushing double-, triple-, quadruple-baby strollers, kids hanging off them, all wrinkles and flab and bone-deep exhaustion. I'd felt this oppression vicariously when I layered on every item of clothing I had and ventured into Mea She'arim to spend the oven-hot July afternoon sweating buckets under my skirts.

I saw oppression in frumpy clothes because in beautiful clothes I saw freedom. I would not be exaggerating even a little—and in fact I'd probably be lowballing it—to say that if I could have back all the minutes in my life I've spent thinking about how I look, it would be enough time to earn a Ph.D. I'm vain. Not cripplingly so. Not to the point where I can't get away from the mirror or where I don't eat anything or where I lose all perspective entirely and believe vanity is a virtue. I'm vain, and it's not great, but that's what it is. Part of this vanity comes from a genuine love of fashion, which at its best really is a virtuous thing. A hand-stitched Gucci leather satchel made by trained artisans in Italy is hardly just a sack for carting around lip gloss and gum. A coat by Alexander McQueen is art. To wear these things is not just to feel fancy but also to feel joined, however superficially, to something beautiful. What you put on your body is not so different from what you put in your body or cram into your brain. It's an assertion of an individual self. The items in your closet may not be terribly rare—there are lots of Gucci handbags in the world and lots more T-shirts from the Gap—but it's all in how you put them together. An obituary made up of lines from other obituaries is still something materially new, and an outfit made from mass-produced items of clothing is distinct and consequential too. I don't mean to get too highfalutin here: Fashion is ultimately just a lot of *stuff*. But I love stuff. I'm a girl in America in the twenty-first century, and, damn it, a pretty dress makes me feel alive.

So where was my dress? Here was my dress, under my blazer and over my leggings, which, yeah, were made of leather for no other reason than because it looks good. Put that in your shofar and blow it!

I managed to live in Crown Heights for weeks before making eye contact with a single woman on the street, which was easy enough since I avoided them and they avoided me. "Oppressed," I thought as we passed each other. "Whore," they thought—or I thought for them. It wasn't a great feeling, being such an obvious interloper, but there's always been comfort for me in playing the outcast. I read my primer in feminism and thought of myself as a feminist in the broadest sense, but I wanted nothing to do with the feminist movement just as I wanted nothing to do with Girl Scouts or organized religion or doubles tennis in high school. I didn't run off and campaign for Barack Obama like half the people I knew, and I didn't move to Williamsburg and dress like a hipster, and I never went to college football games or joined Tumblr or played for the *Wall Street Journal* softball team. I wanted no consciousness of membership in any class, and if sometimes that meant feeling ostracized, fine. I thought of myself as a smooth cylinder with no real parts for joining, not like a puzzle piece or a strip of Velcro. You can put a cylinder next to other objects and there can be closeness, even connection, but if you really got down to it, in my view we were all just glasses in a cupboard, separate and distinct. When you're lonely as a kid, as I was, this is one way of making sense of the world. Over time, it grew into a protective shield; and it's turned out to be a really swell defense mechanism, wonderful for getting over breakups, since you can just remind yourself you've always been in it alone. Whether this is a terrific way of going through life is another question.

At the moment, the questions I was asking instead were: Which designer will make Michelle Obama's dress for the White House state dinner honoring Indian prime minister Manmohan Singh? Who will replace Diane Sawyer on *Good Morning America*? On a scale of one to ten, how much did you love Proenza Schouler's fall collection, because I would say, like, eight? I spent my workdays researching these issues and writing up articles with what I found. My feeling was that these were all good questions. My efforts to answer them gave some people a few minutes of entertaining reading, and maybe on occasion even made them laugh, and that was a worthwhile-enough thing to do.

It was a relief to get to Manhattan, to these worthwhile-enough pursuits, after my run-in with the *tsnius* police, and I put off coming back to Crown Heights for as long as possible. The glorious fall morning had turned into a blustery night by the time I got back, and a strong wind pushed me south on Kingston Avenue. I leaned backward, straining to stay upright, rapping quietly under my breath and avoiding eye contact.

At some point, I felt a heavy object graze my right ear.

I froze, my pulse racing: The long-anticipated assault was finally here! Despite years of warning, I was ill prepared. No sneakers, no whistle, no introductory-level jujitsu. All I had to lean back on was Jay-Z in my ear and a lingering indifference to life itself.

I looked behind me, expecting to face the villain: a gang of hoodlums or maybe a caped evildoer. Instead I saw a fat Lubavitcher teen cursing the heavens. I looked forward and saw his black felt hat skipping down the street, carried by the wind. Without thinking, I took off after it, sprinting down Kingston Avenue in my heels and my leggings and my too-short Diane von Furstenberg shift. I looked back for a moment and saw the yeshiva bocher waddling after me.

A block later, I caught up to the hat and tried to trap it under the right toe of my boot. In doing so, I lost my balance and skidded to the ground, where I landed on the brim of the hat and skinned my left knee on the pavement, tearing my legging and scraping skin. But I had the hat. I held it up at the boy, who huffed and puffed his way over, grabbed it and then scuttled away without looking at me. My heart was pounding in my ears. It was a nice reminder the thing still worked.

I got up, dusted myself off and began to make my way home. I heard footsteps coming up behind me and turned to see a young rabbi with short curly hair and a long red beard. He introduced himself as Yitzhak.

"I saw what you did," he said. "That was very kind."

"Oh, um, thanks," I said, looking down at my knee.

"Are you new to the neighborhood?"

"Yes."

"And how do you find it?"

"Different," I said and then, feeling guilty, added, "nice."

He smiled.

"Are you Jewish?" he asked.

"Yes," I said. "Only, not very."

"Not very is enough."

He gave me his telephone number and invited me to join him and his family for shabbas.

I pictured Yitzhak's house on shabbas. Did his poor, bedraggled wife spend the day slaving over a hot stove while half a dozen children under the age of four ran around screaming? Did they look at each other like strangers across the table, since his thoughts were devoted to God and hers were confined to housework and babies? Did they collapse of exhaustion in separate beds as soon as the last wailing infant was coaxed to sleep? What did they talk about? Were they happy?

You meet a new person, and within seconds, you tell yourself a story of his life. I knew nothing about Yitzhak and his wife, and I knew nothing about the domestic customs of the Lubavitcher community in Crown Heights. If I'd just passed him on the street on a regular day, I'd have taken him for one more religious nut. If he'd struck up a conversation, I'd have assumed he was just trying to save another sinner, rack up one more point on the big Lubavitcher scoreboard of Jews. But in the moment, none of the familiar story lines seemed to fit. I said good-bye to Yitzhak, and as I watched him make his way in the direction of home, I felt the wind blow straight through my body, as if I weren't there. I was cold and alone, and it was midnight, and I was on a street corner in Crown Heights, where absolutely no one wanted me to be. My knee hurt. My outfit was ruined. I was tired of fighting. Yitzhak had been so kind, I felt myself wishing him a happy life. So as I trudged home, I wrote him a different story. I imagined his house, warm and cozy, the dining room lit by candles, pots heating up on the stove. His rosy-cheeked children were asleep in their beds. His wife, played in my mind by British actress Emily Blunt, was kind and bright-eyed and full of vim. Underneath her shapeless clothes was a bodacious figure, and when he looked at her, he thought, "You are everything to me."

I never went over for shabbas, never met his kids or his wife, and never saw Yitzhak again. But I think often of their family, or my imaginary version of it, because it was in that moment that I discovered a brand-new category of New York City fantasy. It was the first time I imagined that a family might be a nice thing to have.

What's great about wanting clothes or party invitations or pretty hair is that those desires simplify life. You walk by a window and look in and say, "That's *me.*" But looking a certain way only makes you look a certain way, when the genuine longing is within: for the confidence that is the real source of beauty or the calm that actually makes a person cool. In that moment, what I wanted was to feel like I was a solid presence on the planet, a barrier to the wind. And it wasn't a matter of replacing my leggings or buying a heavier coat. I wanted the warm house and the soup on the stove and even, so help me God, the babes in their beds—only I didn't want that particularly either. What I wanted was the essence of it, running like marrow through my bones.

You meet a new person and tell yourself a story about him, except it turns out the stories are never about anyone else. They are always about you.

The Jilted-Lady Beat

I hate the holidays. I might have loved the holidays if I were Yitzhak with three precious kiddies and Emily Blunt waiting for me at home. But I was me, and all I had back at the apartment were an irritable rabbi, twelve still-packed boxes of clothes and mounting evidence of a mouse problem. Holidays for most people are an exciting opportunity to gather with loved ones in front of the family hearth, to exchange gifts, to argue and to realize how truly fantastic your regular life is, because, if nothing else, at some point the holidays end and you get to return to it. For me, they conjured less warm feelings. As a kid, I spent the holidays in my bedroom, mostly, watching Christmas movies on television and wishing I were at school. More recently, Chad had used them as an opportunity to suggest desired physical and behavioral improvements. One year, for my birthday, he got me a yoga mat and the entrance fee for a single yoga class. Another year, for our anniversary, I got an espresso machine he'd really been wanting and a quick lesson in how to make him a cappuccino. For our last Hanukkah together, I'd given him a leather jacket, and he'd given me a paperback book called *834 Kitchen Quick Tips*, with the price cut out of the back cover. "Some people are just bad at gift giving," I would tell myself in lieu of considering the larger implications. I didn't want to be one of those girls who cared too much about material things, so I just pretended not to be hurt.

Thanksgiving has always been my one pleasurable day in this otherwise dismal season because Thanksgiving, like marijuana and pregnancy, is a free pass to overeat. I am a serious, rapturous, almost religious consumer of food, and if I hadn't inherited my father's metabolism, I would be the size of a Mack truck. It's never fun to get too psychological about one's excesses, because dissecting a pleasure inevitably diminishes it. But it's true that on the many long afternoons and evenings I spent in my room as a child, I consumed an enormous quantity of Häagen-Dazs chocolate ice cream. For breakfast in the mornings, I ate two chocolate-covered Entenmann's doughnuts, and for dinner at night I sometimes ate two more. The weeks after my breakup were the first and last times I was unable to eat.

"Nothing tastes as good as skinny feels," said the supermodel Kate Moss when asked by a journalist for her personal motto.

"I am always either guilty or hungry," said human coat

hanger Helen Gurley Brown, the great feminist and founder of *Cosmopolitan*.

"I'll eat when I'm dead," said Daphne Guinness, the beer heiress.

"You need to learn that sugar is not nourishment," says Madeleine, who once climbed Mount Kilimanjaro and probably loves the taste of kale.

I will never be as hungry as Helen Gurley Brown, as skinny as Kate Moss or as supremely rational and well-adjusted as my shrink. I live for sugar the way certain insufferable people live for the gym, and I've made my peace with that. Call it a crutch, call it an addiction, call it the sad solace of a lonely girl. It's just the way I am. I get real joy from carbohydrates. I love cake like a fat kid loves cake.

Of course, the only thing better than cake is turkey, stuffing, mashed potatoes, Brussels sprouts, gravy, two kinds of cranberry sauce, green bean casserole, sweet potatoes with little marshmallows melted on top, apple pie, cherry pie, pumpkin pie—and cake. Which is why Thanksgiving is the most religious day of my calendar year.

By the time Thanksgiving rolled around, I had plunged headlong into the period following an epic and well-deserved breakup that Nora Ephron called the "warm bath of innocent victimization." It was by then abundantly clear that I had done the right thing, the fact of which our friends—I had come away with basically all of them—were at pains to remind me. Someday, they promised, I would barely remember the turd I had dated all those years. I came more slowly to this realization and even felt sad for Chad in the early days. This despite his habit of sending me long e-mail apologies, all of which fell somewhere short of genuine contrition. "If I could cut my heart out without killing myself, I would," he wrote the afternoon after our breakup. So what was the point then, exactly? If I could forget he ever existed without suffering the unwelcome side effects of brain damage, I thought, I would nuke my hippocampus. But there was no point in writing. The last time Chad and I spoke was the weekend before Thanksgiving, when he sent me a long letter complaining that his parents wouldn't subsidize his plane ticket home, and I asked him to please never write me again.

Cosmo had never celebrated Thanksgiving. He had never even tasted turkey and he longed to, so I invited him to join some of my friends and me for a group dinner at a large loft in downtown Brooklyn. It was an orphans' gathering, a random group of people with no families or nowhere else to go. The hosts were Allegra, the owner of an art gallery on the Lower East Side, and her boyfriend, Forrest, a chef and restaurateur whose entire body was covered in tattoos. Cosmo had to work at the copy shop that day, since Lubavitchers, who have enough regularly scheduled holidays, don't exactly fall all over themselves to celebrate one time four hundred years ago when a bunch of Puritans had a feast. Via a few quick e-mails, Cosmo and I arranged to meet at Allegra's later. We weren't exactly friendly at this point, but we were, in a way, dear friends. This is a strange thing that happens to two people thrown together

in moments of mutual disarray. It's like being the last two survivors on a boat that's just been ransacked by pirates. You have
to learn how to steer the thing before you have time to develop
a rapport.

It was overcast and windy outside on Thanksgiving morning, the kind of day that feels much colder than it actually is.
I slept late and soundly on my new Sealy Posture Premier.
Around two I pulled on three sweaters and dragged myself
downtown for a long soak in the tub of righteousness. Allegra
met me at the door to the apartment, an open beer in one
hand. I handed over a six-pack of Brooklyn Lager and settled
on the couch next to Forrest's parents, who were watching
football.

Allegra is a New York City girl, born and bred, but she
could just as easily have parachuted in from Majorca. She's
always wearing a bright red vintage dress and big turquoise
earrings, or a bright green vintage dress and rainbow-striped
vintage mules, or a yellow vintage dress and a very large
custom-made black-feathered hat. She is a little bit proper
and a little bit profane, and she laughs outrageously in a way
that makes you feel like you've performed some wild feat just
in saying something funny. The best laughs, like Allegra's,
blow up like bubbles around everyone who's in on the joke.
This, to me, is the holy grail of human connection, and Allegra
is a wonder at it. You draw a little circle around people and say,
"No one else gets this, just us."

Dinner itself was on a narrow wooden table in a large ban-
quet hall with an antelope skull mounted on the far wall. There

were two wood-burning stoves in the corner and a few scattered animal pelts on the raw cement floor. The food had already been served when Cosmo arrived, and I was already reeling from two strong Manhattans. There were two fires going and the room was toasty, but even with the cocktails, I couldn't get warm. Cosmo called from the subway stop, lost, and I went outside and performed Beyoncé choreography in the street so he could see where we were. He brought a bottle of kosher wine. When he entered, he said quiet hellos to the large group and said no to dinner, claiming he felt full.

All I felt from the moment the night started was a humming in my ears and a deep coldness somewhere in my gut that tryptophan and whiskey couldn't warm. When I called to retrace my steps the next day, Allegra told me it had been a perfectly lovely night, and I believed her. But I hadn't been aware of any such thing at the time. I floated around the room, turning circles, mouthing the words to the music playing in the background and listening attentively as one after another person said how much better off I was now. I drifted in and out of conversations, heard Cosmo arguing with one guy about agriculture in Scotland, telling another about G-dcast, this really swell podcast his friend produced that analyzed each week's Torah portion. "You can find it on Facebook." "Oh yeah?" At some point I looked over and Cosmo was devouring a plate of food, with nonkosher turkey that had been slow-cooked underneath a layer of bacon. He looked ecstatic.

"Cosmo, do you want to know what you're eating?" I asked.

"Let's leave it a mystery," he said.

I imagined the two of us leaving together, trudging through Brooklyn late at night, to the subway, to the apartment we shared, and in doing so, I lost my balance and collapsed into a chair. The shape of it all was so familiar. You go to a dinner, you chitchat, you have dessert, and then you go to your home with your man. It is the organizing principle of adult life, but in this case, it felt like insanity. It's so disorienting to look around and see the world unchanged, and the only difference is that you are completely unrecognizable, frozen under three sweaters, in what was supposed to be your prime.

A few weeks later, a census form appeared under Cosmo and my door, and I looked at it for fifteen solid minutes before tearing it up and throwing it out. That winter did not seem like the time to register consciousness, it seemed like the time to obliterate it. It turned out much of New York felt the same way. A year hence, because of dismally low participation and questionable efforts of census workers to try to force people to count themselves, New York Senator Charles Schumer mounted an effort to invalidate the results. Forget 2010— before it even got going, we were all trying to.

"Are you happy?" Cosmo asked, trying to catch my eyes. "Are you happy on the inside or on the outside?"

"Of course I'm happy, Cosmo!" I said, pirouetting, avoiding his gaze. "I'm always happy." As I said this I realized just how untrue it was, and that realization had the same effect as Cosmo's armpit-twist rug-burn jujitsu move that had sent me tumbling to the ground. Except this time the flight response won out. I looked around the room and then I fled, leaving Cosmo there by himself, happily smoking hand-rolled cigarettes beside one of the wood-burning stoves. I ditched him before dessert. I said good-bye to Allegra and slipped out to the street. I hailed a cab and took it into Manhattan, to a giant loft in Soho, to another Thanksgiving—invitation only, no guests allowed— hosted by Dave, a high-fashion photographer I barely knew, and attended by eight models, two other photographers and Dave's mom. When I got there, dinner was over. Dave's mom had left. Bowls—still brimming with mashed potatoes, stuffing, cranberry sauce, yams, salad and Brussels sprouts—and giant serving plates of turkey were out on the table. Here, no one was much into eating. Here, the spirit of Kate Moss compelled everyone to pack into the bathroom every hour or so and pass around a tiny baggie of cocaine. I would've loved to join in on these clown-car coke binges, but I had never done cocaine, and this was plainly obvious to everyone there, since they all seemed to rise and disappear in unison, as if beckoned by a high-pitched whistle I couldn't hear. No one invited me along. Profligacy being its own kind of destiny, I stayed behind on the couch and worked my way through a pecan pie.

Someone had set up a karaoke machine on the giant flat-panel TV, and two Russian models, both named Svetlana, were singing their way through the Smiths. A British model and actor named Alex, an old friend with ice-blue eyes and a Ken-doll torso, found a bicycle somewhere and was pedaling it leisurely up and down the hallway. Everyone knew my story somehow; and over the course of the evening, each person at the party came up to offer their condolences, to tell me about their own experiences cheating or being cheated on. I had a vegan oatmeal cookie. At some point, Alex's girlfriend, a Korean supermodel named Eileen, took a microphone from one of the Svetlanas and told me a long story about a five-year relationship she'd gotten into when she was fifteen, and how the guy had cheated on her seven times, and how she caught him by waiting outside a theater and surprising him when he emerged hand in hand with his ex-girlfriend. No one knew why she spoke into a microphone, but it was a good story and we were all crying by the end. The moral was that my misery, while acute, was also banal. It didn't make the experience better or worse for me to hear this message broadcast over a top-of-the-line speaker system.

The first time I woke up, I was in bed next to the one who went by "Sveta." She was sleeping in a full-length ball gown she'd worn to this, her first Thanksgiving. I was wearing boxers and someone's Harvard T-shirt. The second time I woke up, it was because Alex was giving me a kiss on the forehead. "Open up," he said. I did. He popped a Valium from a silver blister pack and placed it gently down in the center of my tongue. Then he handed me a cup of vodka, and I took a quick swallow.

"Just a little Val-y, dolly," he said. "One left, pumpkin. Just for you."

THE THIRD TIME I woke up it was Friday. I was sleeping on the couch in the front part of the apartment, under a small

chenille area rug. I woke because Edward, my boss, was calling my cell phone. Edward was the executive editor of the
Daily Beast, a Jewish lawyer from Tennessee who had worked
for many years as an editor at the *Wall Street Journal*. He was
the one who had interviewed me for a job at the *Beast*. When
I came, I was wearing a very carefully selected outfit designed
to make me look as much as possible like a character from *The
Devil Wears Prada*: a black dress, black stockings, and black
five-inch platform wedge shoes, which put me up around six
foot three. Edward, I discovered that first time we met, is not
a tall man. About a foot separated us, with me in my silly
heels, and I spent the duration of our interview praying for
someone to come and saw me off at the knees.

"Do you know who Tiger Woods is?" he asked when I
rasped hello.

"Yes, I know who Tiger Woods is," I said too authoritatively.

Edward laughs like he's throwing something at you. It
announces his presence in a building—a zip code—with the
clarity and reach of an air raid siren. He's clever and calm, and
the way he draws a circle around two people is to speak as if
everyone else on the planet were an absolute drunk buffoon
and that you are the only sane ones left. My colleague Jacob, a
muscle-bound entertainment writer, says that in journalism, a
person generally has one of two dispositions: either he reacts
to every piece of news with shock, or he reacts to everything
with amusement. Edward is among the latter group, and it
was always fun to get an assignment from him, since work
became an exercise in plumbing other people's idiotic depths.

Edward was calling because a terrible thing had happened to Tiger Woods, the greatest golfer who ever lived. Woods and his wife, Swedish model Elin Nordegren, had two precious children, a nice home in Florida and around a billion dollars in accrued and expected income from a raft of lucrative sponsorship deals. Until Thanksgiving 2009, Woods was easily the most boring professional athlete in America. He barely gave interviews, and when he did, they were full of bland sound bites about his love for the game and his beautiful family—who cares? What Elin reportedly discovered on Thanksgiving Day was that the most boring professional athlete in America had a truly Olympian taste for rough sex with cocktail waitresses. In his years on the road, according to news reports that would emerge in the coming weeks, Woods amassed more than a dozen mistresses. These included a porn star, several dubiously tasked nightclub employees and one considerably older woman, whom the press dubbed "Tiger's cougar." When Elin discovered this, after brief cell-phone contact with the puffy-lipped woman the press would dub Tiger's "alpha mistress," her brain did not desert her body. It pointed her in the direction of her husband's clubs, one of which she reportedly took to the family Escalade, Tiger cowering within.

When the news broke that tryptofantastic Friday, the Woods scandal captivated a sleepy nation. We were all bored senseless by the other news of the day—health care reform, the wars in Afghanistan and Iraq, the interminable recession—but how much fun is a storybook marriage collapsing luridly before your eyes! The story had everything anyone could ever want: hubris, fake breasts, a fallen idol, his wronged wife. While strumpet after strumpet paraded before the media at press conferences in the weeks that followed, Elin did nothing. It was mesmerizing. She moved about Florida like a wood nymph. She spent her days driving back and forth to the gas station and to her children's school. In the six months that elapsed between the alleged Thanksgiving incident and the announcement of their preliminary divorce settlement, virtually the only pictures paparazzi managed to get were of her in yoga pants and sunglasses, standing calmly next to her SUV. I looked in the reflective coating of her sunglasses in the pictures of her that came across the wires and thought: What is going *on* in there?

It is only relatively recently that sex scandals have become such big business for American journalism. British tabloids figured it out first, chasing Princess Diana into an early grave, and still do it best. We Puritans were slower to catch on, a delay that made it possible for a college student in the early twenty-first century to imagine a journalism career that would never involve hours spent in search of the phone number of the ex-wife of the gay former governor of New Jersey. Everyone blames Gary Hart, who in 1987 challenged the media to report on his personal life while he was running for president, then seemed shocked to be caught with his mistress, for the initial breach. The Clinton scandal a decade hence turned infidelity into an entire category of political journalism. The Woods scandal, breaking like dawn over my post-Thanksgiving hangover, would turn it into a legitimate business proposition for a slew of struggling new media outlets. Entire publications survived for months on Tiger Woods, following every minor development and every false lead with surgical precision. Paparazzi provided live-action video of the train wreck. This sort of attention is a condition of celebrity in the modern era, but it was jacked up to the highest setting for Woods. Every time pop star Britney Spears went for a microwavable burrito at her local gas station, swarms of photographers recorded the trip for posterity, and this went tenfold for Tiger's many supposed mistresses. These pictures and videos helped keep countless news organizations in business at a time when "news," in the traditional sense, had ceased to be much of a moneymaker. We made photo galleries with these pictures and used them to boost the Web traffic of the *Daily Beast.* We wrote stories pivoting off minor details in the Woods saga, as if contained within the collapse of this marriage were a thousand koans, an infinitely applicable guide to human life. What is Elin's crisis-management strategy here? Why don't famous women get caught up in sex scandals the way men do? How have wronged women learned from the media coverage of other wronged women? I wrote all these essays and more in the weeks that followed. It was beyond meta. It was a metastasis.

Even the altruists among us—the hospice nurses, the bone marrow donors—must have mornings when they wake up under a chenille area rug and say, "What the hell am I doing with my life?" To be young and to desire a unique and worthwhile existence on this planet is basically to fight a feeling of pointlessness every minute of the day. You fix a thousand cleft palates and there are millions more you could never get to, and what's to stop those smiling kids from dying of AIDS a year later or chopping each other to bits in some incomprehensible war or growing up to be the lowest kind of human life, anonymous Internet commenters who spend their afternoons trolling websites and leaving messages like "Who cares?" Alternately, you write stories for a living, and maybe occasionally you say something that passes for genuine insight, but then the rest of the time it's just you and Elin Nordegren and the designer of Michelle Obama's latest gown in the great Internet traffic jam of hell. To be young and to desire a unique and worthwhile existence as a journalist in the age of search engine optimization—when the ultimate goal of every endeavor is to lure as many anonymous commenters as possible, to get as many odious Internet aggregators to link to your little bit of bother on the Tiger Woods debacle—felt, that winter, after my entire life collapsed, like one more aspect of an already extinct dream.

In the months that followed that first phone call with Edward, I interviewed Dina McGreevey, ex-wife of former New Jersey governor Jim McGreevey, who resigned and came out as a "gay American" in 2004. I attended an intimate ladies lunch with Jenny Sanford, ex-wife of doomed South Carolina governor Mark Sanford, who told everyone he was going hiking on the Appalachian Trail in the spring of 2009 and instead went to visit his Argentinean lover, to whom he wrote long letters about the pleasures of farmwork. Both women had written books about their marital struggles, and Sanford signed a copy of hers for me at the end of our lunch, which occurred at an empty midtown restaurant at the beginning of a blizzard; Lou Dobbs sat two tables away. From my little desk in my big candy-colored office, I tapped out these stories in two hours or less. "Commerce, not art," I told myself. And when I got lucky, lots of people read my commerce and left a note about how dumb or ugly I was.

For months, beginning that Friday, I wrote almost exclusively about wronged women. I did none of this out of sympathy or because it brought me deep satisfaction, but because it was good for "clicks." These stories begat television appearances, which begat more stories in this vein, until I was fully consumed on what I began to call the "jilted-lady beat." It's not a perfect place to be, the jilted-lady beat. It doesn't soothe the soul. But it was a means to an end. In the short term, that end was to be a productive, functioning member of the world again. In the longer view, the end was murkier, and so I avoided the longer view.

At the frenzied peak of jilted-lady season, I began going to the Boom Boom Room, a self-consciously decadent, exclusive nightclub on the top floor of a new hotel called the Standard. Boom Boom—or Booms or Le Boom—was a soaring space, yellow lit and dark, vaulted eighteen stories above Manhattan, with wide leather banquettes poured like thick caramel into semiprivate nooks. The front door was covered in soft beige leather and the blond-colored carpeting was spread like batter on the floor. There were two fireplaces in the far corners of the room, and it was hot inside, dizzying. Boom Boom was a warp zone, except instead of throwing you back into another era, it dropped you into a coffee table book about nightlife in New York, with carefully chosen pictures from big nights at Studio 54, Max's Kansas City, the old Don Hill's. There wasn't an original experience to be had at Boom, but you could pretty enjoyably imitate a fabulous scene from the past, like being on a "nightclub" ride at a Disney theme park. That wasn't Mick Jagger and Jerry Hall lounging in the corner, but it was Marc Jacobs and his boyfriend, Lorenzo Martone, in pretty much the same languid pose. Instead of Rick Hilton there was Nicky Hilton, instead of Ivana Trump there was Ivanka. Madonna still occasionally stopped by. One night Chris Noth, the actor who played Mr. Big in *Sex and the City*, crammed into the elevator car next to me and we rode up side by side, surrounded by his entourage. Sometimes you come so close to your childhood vision of happiness that you can smell it. In my experience, it almost always smells like a cologne strip in a glossy magazine.

I clicked up to Boom on python stilettos for the first time ever a few weeks after Thanksgiving, flanked by girlfriends, determined to shed a skin. An old Michael Jackson song was playing, loud, when we got there, and as I took my first step onto the plush carpet, the club closed around me like a padded cell. Everywhere there were shiny skinny girls in miniskirts, their hair pony-straight and glossy. With them in clusters were boys in jackets and jeans, with the carefully mussed look of the young and well-to-do. It used to be people, even rich people, looked different. But now, in New York, we've cracked the code. We know the workouts to make you skinny, the chemicals for your hair, the medicines for your skin and the clothes for your figure. Now all girls are hot and all boys are cool. It's Memory Game, only instead of rabbis, everyone looks like a Hilton sister.

We didn't even make it to the bar before a handsome darkhaired stranger came up and said hello. He knew one of my girlfriends. He kissed me on the cheek and told me his name was—whatever. What was my name? he asked—whatever. We talked like this in the loud club for no more than a minute—"[Something]?" "[Unrelated]"—like people shouting through pillows. Then he grabbed my hand and said, "Come." I'm not really a girl to whom men just say "come." I'm more of a girl to whom men say things like "Wow, you're tall," or "What did you say your name was again?" But he said "Come" and so I followed, following his deep voice into the dark center of the club. We ended up in a hallway lined with mirrors, which picked up light from some untraceable source and sent it pinging around, glinting off the specks of mica in the black marble floor. The mirrors turned out to be bathroom doors. We went in one. The far wall of the tiny bathroom was a three-foot-wide window stretching all the way from the polished black floor up fourteen feet to the mirrored ceiling. The window looked north over Manhattan, over the Hudson and up along the west side of the city, across the low brick brownstones of the Village and Chelsea, to the Empire State Building and the Chrysler Building and the skyscrapers of midtown. You could see New Jersey too. You could almost see stars.

I was dressed in my shortest possible dress, *tsnius* be damned, and in that moment, I was nothing under my clothes. Not a journalist, not a New Yorker, no one's girlfriend, nothing. I pressed my nose against the cold window and felt the whole slick, smooth, black shining whirl of the club melt away behind me. The noise melted and the people melted and the path that brought me there melted. Amnesia set in, and for a moment I floated alone over everything. There was no work and no loss, no holidays and no Tiger Woods. No youth and no striving. No point and also no need for one. There was only this girl in her dress and the blinking lights below. Just me and the city: barest bones.

The nameless stranger produced a tiny bag of cocaine.

"I've never done this before," I said.

"I don't believe you," he said.

The thing I noticed was that it smelled like lilacs.

When the impulse to feel something, anything, rubs up against the impulse to feel nothing at all, that internal friction creates a kind of warmth. I looked up into the bathroom mirror, deep into my own eyes, and the only thought that entered my head was that my mascara looked spectacular.

"Smile," he said in his butterscotch voice, and thinking he was being sweet, I smiled my loveliest smile, playing Edie Sedgwick at Max's Kansas City, playing the part of a girl to whom strangers at fancy nightclubs say things like "Come." He smiled back. Then he licked his finger, dunked it into the bag of blow, ran it along my gumline, and said, "There. That'll make you feel a little numb."

Chosen People

It was the first night of Hanukkah, two weeks before Christmas, dead in the middle of the dreaded holiday season. I emerged from the subway in Crown Heights at seven o'clock, singing Lily Allen.

You're not big, you're not clever. . . .
Not big whatsoever.

It's a song about ditching a man with a small penis and no money. It filled me with old-fashioned Hanukkah cheer.

The first thing I noticed when I stepped into the frigid air was that, in my absence, Crown Heights had been struck by a daring act of vandalism. Someone, sly devil, had snuck around in broad daylight and spray-painted over a giant advertisement for *It's Complicated*, a forthcoming Nancy Meyers movie starring Alec Baldwin, Steve Martin and Meryl Streep. On the poster, Streep was pictured in bed with Baldwin. It showed Streep and Baldwin naked under the covers, his arm behind her neck, in a dreamy, postcoital pose. His chest was visible— hair, nipples, everything—but only her shoulders were. The strap of a satin camisole dangled low on one arm, presumably displaced by vigorous lovemaking. The vandal, displaying an uncommon bias, had painted over every inch of the angelic Streep, blotting out flesh, camisole, disheveled hair, squinty maternal grin. Swarthy Baldwin was left untouched. At a dinner months hence, some of the younger members of the Lubavitch community would chuckle and shake their heads at the presumed perpetrator: damned *tsnius* police.

Looking up from Baldwin's furry clavicle, I noticed another disturbance in the sleepy nighttime rhythms of the 'chood. The usual phalanx of mitzvah tanks scattered around had exploded in number. The streets were clogged with RVs, mini-vans and rusted-out Volvo station wagons, double-parked as far as the eye could see. Each had a plastic menorah with candle-shaped lightbulbs affixed to the roof and signs wishing every-one a happy Hanukkah. Many had a laminated banner taped to the front bumper, which said "The Time for Your Redemp-tion Is Now!" I stood on Eastern Parkway and watched as the Hasidim piled into their makeshift mitzvah tanks, strapped their children into car seats, held the passenger doors open for their wives, revved up the sputtering engines and pulled out one by one into a parade. It was chilly after the sun went down, but all those fake candles threw off a holiday heat. The Hanuk-kah brigade would spend the next few hours driving around

Manhattan and the outer boroughs, passing out Hanukkah candles and cheap aluminum menorahs to anyone who looked like a Jew and shouting good wishes to anyone who would listen. As I walked home, the cars whizzed by me, and I watched the blur of their signs like a cable news ticker:

"The Time for Your Redemption Is Now!"

. . . "Redemption Is Now!"

. . . "Is Now!" . . . "Now!" . . . "Now!"

It was nearly eleven o'clock when Cosmo got home from jujitsu. Quietly, like a Hanukkah ninja, he moved one of the two red plastic kitchen chairs out into the living room and covered the top of the chair in tin foil. He placed a flimsy aluminum menorah on the chair's seat and put two candles in: one for the first night of Hanukkah and one shammash, or head candle. He began to sing the blessings to himself in a low voice, trying not to disturb me in my room. I came out somewhere in the middle of this whispered observance and seeing it, burst into tears.

We hadn't really spoken much since Thanksgiving, except passing pleasantries. I'd apologized the next day for leaving him stranded at Allegra's, and he'd said not to worry, that the turkey had been delicious. Occasionally he told me about jujitsu, asked if it was okay to wash his uniform in the tub, smoked cigarettes in the window or listened to me talk about work—empty, distancing things. I barely knew Cosmo at this point, but to get to know him was to acknowledge the reality of the situation. It was much easier to just put on pretty clothes and get high.

But there are certain sense memories you cannot deny—less Proustian madeleines, more baseball bats to the face—and one of these, for me, is the smell of cheap candles burning down into a disposable menorah. This combined fire hazard and holy ritual of the contemporary American Jewish faith rockets me back to Hanukkahs of yore, to the fuzzy, cozy footie-pajamaed winter nights of my youth. Hanukkah is a great time to be a Jewish child, possibly the only time of year when other people actually wish they were Jews. In one version of the story (there are always multiple, contradictory versions of Jewish stories), Hanukkah commemorates the rededication of the second Holy Temple in Jerusalem, when a little bit of oil miraculously lasted eight days. On the spectrum of miracles, this strikes me as pretty minor, but for it, Jewish children get eight days of presents, so God bless. In my house as a kid, Hanukkah also meant a precious week of relative peace. My parents cooked latkes together, arguing about oil temperature over a hot stove, while I sat in the living room, shaking my gifts. It was the one time of year we reliably made a fire in the gas-log fireplace, my father holding out one long match and turning the metal key in the side of the chimney that brought the whole illusion to life. When I remember those days I remember them as if through a fog of latke grease and propane, the sepia tone for suburban Jews.

We sang the blessings, all three of us, and then I got to pick one package and open it. There are few moments in life as good as the one right before you open a present. When else is anyone so hopeful and naïve? Even after you've gotten enough presents in life to know that whatever's in the box is probably not as great as you want it to be, you never really stop hoping. Or I hope you don't. The day someone hands me a present and I think *meh* is the day it's all over. If life has wrung you so dry you can't get excited about presents, forget about it.

As a child, I was entranced by the unknown treasures that lay in wait, wrapped in last season's discount Christmas paper, piled before the fake fireplace in our den. What unimaginable joys lurked within? Would the thing inside bounce or make noise or fly? Was it . . . battery operated? Battery-operated toys in my house were about as rare and precious as dry-clean-only clothes: infrequently gifted, judiciously used. Far likelier, for my Hanukkahs, were items I had casually deliberately mentioned I wanted during meanderings with my mother through Monroeville Mall. Would it be the cable-knit Abercrombie & Fitch sweater I'd been coveting (seventh grade), in the powder-blue color that I thought would go nicely with my eyes? Would it be a boom box (fourth grade) or the debut album by Ace of Base (fifth)? Or, oh God oh God, would it be the American Girl doll Molly, the one with the glasses, my American dream girl? (Second grade, and it would also be her school desk with the little pencils and notepads, so we could play "quiet nerds" together in my room.) Would it be a book? (Yes, every year it would be a book.)

When I saw Cosmo whispering the Hanukkah blessings to himself, I shrank down into the twelve-year-old with the freshly unwrapped powder-blue sweater that matches her eyes, for whom this solitude would have been the gravest, deepest offense. You simply can't be alone on Hanukkah, even though it's really a little nothing of a holiday. On the scale of Jewish holy days—and there are many Jewish holy days—Hanukkah is about as important to Hasids like Cosmo as Kwanzaa is to Hasids like Cosmo. But try telling that to a godless twelve-year-old who just spent the day watching *A Christmas Story* on loop and who knows, to her very core, that something potentially life-changing sat in front of the fire.

What can you do under such circumstances? I didn't have any presents hidden away, so I sat down in an armchair and waited until he was done.

"Tell me about your family," I said.

"What's to say, really," he said.

"What did your parents do in Russia?"

"They did what everyone's parents did."

"And what was that?"

"They were rocket scientists."

Every superhero has his own creation mythology, and so does every person who comes to New York. Cosmo cultivated an air of mystery around his upbringing, as if he emerged whole and hardened on the streets of Brooklyn, his past a gauzy void. I never bought it. Who knows how alike Cosmo and I actually were, but we had at least this in common: We wanted to find, and so found in each other, a similar pattern of pain and resilience. His parents were geniuses. He grew up alone. His childhood was the fog he drove a tank through.

Cosmo's parents were Jewish, but he grew up in Soviet Russia, so any religious observance was limited. In an act of teenage rebellion, he embraced Orthodoxy. He hooked up with the Lubavitchers and "started getting really into it." He studied the Talmud. He learned about Menachem Mendel Schneerson, read his writings and listened to his speeches. He started to believe, and then he *really* started to believe. Schneerson was captivating. Just maybe, Cosmo thought, this guy is actually the Messiah. He imagined what it would be like to come to America, to live a righteous, holy life in the image of his hero.

By this point, the Berlin Wall had come down, and the mafia was making the most of the power vacuum of the immediate post-Soviet era. One way the mob cemented its place in communities was through charity, and one object of their charity in Moscow was Cosmo. Some of his Lubavitcher friends became friendly with a mobster, who funneled them money for books, supplies and other activities. So what if the provenance of the money was less than pristine? This was Russia in the 1990s, and you took money where you could get it. The mob sent Cosmo off to yeshiva in London.

After another yeshiva in northern Israel, near the Sea of Galilee, Cosmo set out for New York, touching down at JFK with a banged-up suitcase full of black coats, white shirts, tallit, tefillin and a few other personal effects. He came across the Atlantic and found himself transported back in time, into a photostatic re-creation of an eighteenth-century shtetl. He knew some Russian men who'd come over before him, and he quickly made friends at shul. He lived cheaply in a group house owned by a man who was remarkably kind and generous to the boys who rented his rooms. During this period, he survived on two dollars a day.

Every Orthodox Jewish mother prays for a tzaddik: a blessed child, a righteous man, a person whose "merit surpasses his iniquity," in Maimonides's words. Who knows if Cosmo is a true tzaddik, but the Crown Heights Lubavitcher community saw potential. They put him up and fed him. They pooled their money and sent him to rabbinical school in South Africa and yeshiva in New Haven. But instead of going off to lead a congregation somewhere, he tucked his certificates into a prayer book, shoved the prayer book on his shelf, and went to work at Fast Trak. The shop's owner agreed to be his sponsor for a green card, and Cosmo was stuck there until his papers came through. As he explained it to me, Cosmo had been on a two-year "temporary status" awaiting his green card, but it "got suspended pending something or other." Once he got a green card, he could work legally or get government loans for school. He could begin his path to eventually becoming a U.S. citizen. Every possible course of life hinged on those papers, and their delay was both infuriating and convenient, since it put off indefinitely any obligation to choose a path, to return to the fold or embrace the profane. His was a life lived twice in deferment—awaiting the Messiah to usher him into the next world and the United States government to accept him into this one.

Hasidic men spend their lives studying Torah. The best become great scholars, sage old men peering out through thick bifocals, dispensing the wisdom of millennia. The flip side of

Orthodoxy is that it keeps all adherents, even the whitest beards among them, in a state of perpetual childhood. You don't have to choose what you eat, the rules of kashruth tell you. You don't have to try out pick-up lines at bars, the community will find you a bride. Whatever parents you had to begin with are, in a way, incidental. The religion is your mother and father. Anytime there is a question about how you should think or behave, the answer is in a book.

Three years before I met him, Cosmo's mother had confessed to a suspicion that she may have been adopted. The book says that a person is Jewish if his mother is Jewish—if and only if. If Cosmo's mother was adopted, she might not be Jewish, which meant he might not be Jewish, which meant—the dominos all collapsed from there. The only areas of life it wouldn't invalidate were his employment status at Fast Trak and his slow progress in jujitsu. Cosmo begged his mother to investigate her lineage, but she declined. Strictly speaking, and there is no other manner of speech to a Hasidic rabbi, given those circumstances, Cosmo should have begun a conversion process, just to be safe, to absolutely guarantee he was a Jew— if not Chosen by God then chosen by his own damn self. Orthodox conversion is a pain in the ass, though, even for someone who's already a rabbi. Cosmo wrestled with whether to go through with it, going back and forth for years. Finally, shortly before I moved in, he decided: No. If he was a Jew, he was a Jew, and if not, not. But at thirty years old, too much of life had already passed to be a slave to technicality.

These were Cosmo's circumstances when my e-mail arrived

in his in-box. He had followed the Messiah to New York, but the Messiah was dead and showed no signs of coming back. And now Cosmo was stuck in a kind of purgatory. He felt trapped in his job, waylaid in Crown Heights, but couldn't just go on taking comfort in the certainty that at least he was still a rabbi, at least still a Jew.

"Do you think you'll ever speak to your mother again?"

"Eventually," he said. "There'll be a wedding, children."

"Really?"

He flashed a rubber-band smile.

"Have you ever heard of Philip Larkin?" I asked.

"No."

"He has a poem I like called 'This Be the Verse,'" I said. Cosmo made his way over to the oak table, sat on top of it and began rolling a cigarette. He paused, looked at me and lowered his black-plastic-frame glasses an inch down on his nose as if to say, "Continue." While he smoked, I recited, clumsily, from memory.

They fuck you up, your mum and dad.
They may not mean to, but they do.

It's a short, rhyming poem by a known anti-Semite about how one generation of parents passes all their bullshit down to the next, and adds "some extra, just for you." The moral is to get away from home as soon as possible and never dare to reproduce.

"Where did you come up with that?" Cosmo asked flatly.

. . .

ONE OF THE BEST THINGS I learned in school was to memorize poetry. My memory used to be terrific, and now it is increasingly terrible, no doubt hampered by trips to the Boom Boom Room over the course of the months that followed. But buried somewhere among the refuse, alongside dialogue from every episode of *Sex and the City* and the phone numbers of several childhood friends, are scattered fragments of James Merrill, William Butler Yeats, Emily Dickinson, Alexander Pope—whatever happened to stick.

The person who told me to memorize poetry is also the person who taught me most of what I know about love and death, sex and jealousy, and the stories people tell themselves about happiness. Harold Bloom was in his seventies by the time I met him—frail, in poor health, terrified of spiders, unable to sleep, confined largely (literally) to the butterscotch-color leather lounge chair in his study. Bloom was a titan in every sense, an intellectual colossus, poetry scholar, and author of such works as *The Western Canon* and *How to Read and Why*. In *The Invention of the Human*, he argued that Shakespeare's characters were not just drawn from life, they drew it—that Hamlet, in a fashion, taught us how to be ourselves. In *The Anxiety of Influence*, he inspired a generation of literary critics to use the tools of psychoanalysis. In person, Bloom was a monstrous, sorrowful figure, with the kindest face I've ever seen, large tufting eyebrows and a forehead permanently shaped into deep furrows of concern. He was always on the verge of tears.

Professor Bloom taught humanities at Yale. I first approached him as a sophomore, shortly after he wrote a piece for the *Wall Street Journal* calling the Harry Potter book series a scourge. *Harry Potter and the Sorcerer's Stone*, the first movie adaptation of the series, had just come out, and if Bloom would watch the film with me, I thought, I could write up the story and sell it to someone. Who knew how Bloom might respond to such a request, but I suspected he wouldn't be game. When you're a journalist—or, as I was at that stage, merely aspiring to be one—you spend your life facing down almost certain rejection. People should really never speak to reporters. We rarely have their interests at heart. The impulse to grant an interview, when it is not in service of some greater social good, basically amounts to a character flaw. It's hard to deny the little voice inside every journalist that says "Why bother?" since there's no good reason someone as brilliant as Professor Bloom would want to spend even a few of his precious minutes on the planet speaking to me. But I was bold and reckless then. When you're eighteen, it's easy to think of reasons people will say yes. I found Bloom's telephone number in the phone book and spent half an hour summoning the courage to call. I imagined him shouting at me for wasting his time, slamming the phone down or worse. Ten times, at least, I rehearsed my pitch, then dialed with a shaky finger, my heart thumping in my chest.

He answered the phone on the first ring. "Yes? Hello?" His voice was quiet and urgent, as if he'd spent the better part of his adult life alone at the bottom of a mine shaft and was just giving up hope of being rescued.

"Hi! Yes, hi, Professor Bloom!" I shouted into the phone, as if his hearing were impaired, which it was not. I stumbled loudly through my pitch.

"Ah, my child," he whispered back. No, of course, he wouldn't come to the theater with me—he couldn't fit into the seats. But if I brought over a VCR and a copy of the film, he would endure a screening in his living room. He said I had a "sweet voice," and he would be happy to meet me. "Okay!" I yelled and then hung up, ecstatic. Having done nothing except shout at a lonely genius, I felt nevertheless that I had achieved something monumental. I had been discovered. He could *tell*. From my voice.

The following Sunday afternoon, it rained as I hauled the TV-VCR combo I'd bought five years earlier with money from my bat mitzvah to Bloom's Tudor-style home and put on a bootleg copy of the film a friend had bought in Times Square. The whole episode lasted fifteen minutes. Harold and his wife, Jeanne, spent ten of them arguing about her latest health kick—she had recently begun the Atkins diet, which he found foolish—and the last five discussing Richard Wagner's influence on film scores. They quickly forgot the film was playing at all and went about attending to the huge volume of visitors who arrived after me, each evidently "chosen" in his own right. Students streamed through the house, which smelled like the Atkins-approved chicken soup Jeanne was heating on the stove. Eventually, I packed up my television and left.

"Good-bye, little bear," Bloom said, hugging me on my way out the door. "Please do come again."

No one bought my story, but the interaction was enough to fix me in Bloom's mind and gain me admittance to his over-subscribed seminars the following year. I read all of Shakespeare with him and every worthwhile twentieth-century American poet. But really what I did was study Bloom, this monstrously isolated, brilliant man—"The Prophet of Decline," as the *New Yorker* called him once. Beset by "messianic loneliness" and "grandiloquent fatigue," he was a great soul, perhaps the greatest. Bloom was on a slew of medications by the time I made it into his class, one of which caused dry mouth, so he paused often to glug from a large sports water bottle. He wore a monitor on his wrist, which beeped straight through our two-hour sessions, in rhythm with his overfull heart. I lived in fear of it speeding up, like I saw happen so many times on hospital-themed TV shows and like I would experience myself, six years hence, waking each morning to Cosmo's alarm.

Bloom said wild things. "Sailing to Byzantium" was "one of those poems you look at and it instantly gives you an immortal wound." He memorized it as a small child, "as indeed I memorized all of Yeats as a small child." On life: "I find it so hard, when I am awake, not to talk." On death: "I have said in my will that I wish to be cremated and my ashes scattered as indifferently as possible." He occasionally quoted himself. His

favorite "Bloomian aphorism" was "If you don't speak ill of the
dead, then who will?" Bloom had been friendly with Gershom
Scholem, as he had been friendly with "Tommy Pynchon,"
John Ashbery, Paul de Man and pretty much everyone else. He
occasionally brought up one of these luminaries as a footnote.
Pynchon, an anxious man, used to say "Even paranoids have
enemies." Scholem "always spoke in the third person: 'As Scholem said . . .'"

Every kid runs into her parents' limitations at some point,
and for me this had happened on matters of the soul. My parents were great at helping me with math problems—hence
Dictionary's warp-speed ascent through middle school
algebra—but the human stuff was rougher terrain. We didn't
talk about love or death or feelings in my house, and so I
learned about them the way I learned about singing: through
books and movies and magazines. In some respects, this is
terrific, since I learned from the best. But the problem with
it is it's one-directional. There's no experience, no exchange.
It turns you into a vessel, a smooth cylinder with no parts
for joining, just a big hole in the center to fill. When I met
Harold Bloom, it was not so different from when I first
encountered Carrie Bradshaw and her own pink, fluffy kind
of messianic sadness. My reaction was awe and instant devotion. I sat quietly and let them pour everything in.

There's a children's book by P. D. Eastman about a little
bird that hops around to different animals and objects, asking,
"Are you my mother?" I read it countless times as a kid and
only recently recognized it for the breathtakingly profound,

essentially religious text it is. I wrote down everything Bloom said while I was his student and did everything he told us to do, and tried, in this manner, to be a kind of daughter to him—not to be *like* him, exactly, but to be the person he might want me to be. Your first pair of parents makes you, and then you go through life choosing different parents, remaking yourself to look like them. Sometimes the person is an actual person, like your annoyingly sporty shrink, and you have the luxury of interacting with her. Sometimes the person isn't real, is instead the protagonist of a mediocre television series or the prince of Denmark. And sometimes the parent you've chosen up and dies, and you're left with a rabbinical certificate and a job you hate at a photocopy shop in Crown Heights, and then all you've got is some random junk, picked up from somewhere, cluttering your brain.

COSMO SAT ON THE WINDOWSILL, nodding and smoking through the first night of our giftless Hanukkah, in what must have been on one of the most pathetic celebrations a Jewish holiday has ever occasioned: no latkes, no family, no singing, no dancing, no joy.

"I don't think Judaism is working for me anymore," he said.

And now: no Judaism.

He went on. "It's a marvelous religion, if you're looking. It's grand. It has facets. It has colors. You know how everyone needs a father figure? Judaism says: 'Here. Don't worry. We

know how the world works.' It's awesome." Except he pronounced it *oowahsome*, drawing the word out to three syllables
as if he were a native Brooklynite who grew up shouting this
sort of thing at Mets games. "But I need something else."

"Wow," I said. "That's big."

"Don't worry," he said. "I'm seventy-five percent sure I'll
come back to it."

If I had to put a number on it, I would have said I was about
75 percent sure I would go back to Manhattan at some point,
get a new apartment, fall in love again, ease back into the
broader outlines of my old life. But maybe I wouldn't! It was a
tantalizing prospect. Maybe I would run off to Buenos Aires
or Majorca or some other place where I might actually get a
tan. Or maybe I would go study an indigenous tribe somewhere like Margaret Mead, and then come back to New York
someday many decades later to deliver a paper before an
esteemed crowd of academics, looking half-feral, wearing a
hopelessly outdated style of jeans. Maybe I would meet a
prince and he would cart me off to Morocco. There really was
no telling. The thing in the shiny package in front of the fireplace might fly or bounce or save my soul. Maybe it would
usher me into a whole new life.

While I have no interest in the miracle of Hanukkah, it is
hard to ignore a hundred signs telling you THE TIME FOR
YOUR REDEMPTION IS NOW NOW NOW. I thought
about Harold Bloom, massive and orphic in his brown leather
chair, and then I looked over at Cosmo, who had left the windowsill and was now sorting out his cigarette papers on our

pleather couch, repeatedly readjusting the glasses on his nose. We sat in silence.

Chosenness is a major concept in contemporary Judaism. Jews believe they are God's beloved nation, gifted with the Torah and destined for greatness. Chosenness is also a fundamental concept in secular society, especially in the achievement-obsessed suburban middle-class prep school world I come from. Get picked for dodgeball, get picked for Yale, get picked by Harold Bloom to schlep a TV over to his house one rainy day. It's all glitter sprinkling down from heaven, making you shine. The brighter you shine, the happier you are. This is what my people believe. But what happens when that belief breaks down? When being chosen loses its luster?

The candles had burned out in Cosmo's cheap menorah, and a waft of singed aluminum floated through the apartment. It could have been a euphoric moment, Cosmo's prison break from Orthodoxy. But it felt more like a somber time, and a scary one. Here was a Hasidic rabbi, a man whose entire adult life had been dictated by the strictures of Judaism, deciding, on the first night of Hanukkah, to give it all up. Would he eat *treyf*? Would he date shiksas? Would he cut off his beard, he wondered, and if so who would do it, and how much would he cut off? The questions were endless.

I looked at Cosmo, motherless son of a motherless mom, and longed to somehow help. It never occurred to me that in that moment he might have felt the same mix of pity and helplessness for me.

Cosmo looked up from the couch.

"Do you know Joseph Brodsky?"

I shook my head.

"He has a poem I like called 'History of the Twentieth Century: A Roadshow.'"

He rolled and lit another cigarette, and then began to recite.

Ladies and gentlemen and the gay!
All ye made of sweet human clay!
Let me tell you: you are okay!

Christmas with
the Goldfarbs

C hristmas Eve dinner was the prix fixe menu at Jean-Georges, one of the finest restaurants in New York. I was with my friend Kate and her mother, Karen, a rich divorcée who arrived, humming, from church, in a wide-brimmed feathered hat. The menu was sautéed scallops, steamed cod, beef tenderloin with horseradish crème and a sampling of seasonal desserts, including a deconstructed apple tart, cinnamon-maple buns, chocolate noodles with vanilla emulsion, something called Textures of Cranberry, plus two $150 bottles of a nice California Pinot Noir. Kate and I went dancing afterward at a club called Avenue, and crawled up to the DJ booth around two a.m., where we met and chatted with an enormous blind pimp in a full-length fur coat, smoking a blunt.

I came home in the middle of the afternoon on Friday, Christmas Day, and found Cosmo and two houseguests sitting in the living room, drinking beer. Michael and Stephanie were both in their twenties, both Orthodox, both wearing jeans. It took a while for me to realize this was a date, since they barely spoke to each other the entire time.

Michael was Cosmo's last roommate and remained one of his only friends. He'd stayed five months in the room that was now mine and then moved to a place on the Lower East Side, where he worked as a computer consultant and sporadically pursued a Ph.D. in applied math. He wore a black zip-up fleece, white socks and a pair of those over-designed hybrid loafers, with the thick black rubber soles, made for men who don't want to buy separate shoes for work, shul and silent Friday afternoon dates. Small wire-frame glasses sat so high on his nose they were nearly contact lenses. The brim of his baseball cap angled sharply down, covering his forehead and most of his eyes. The lights were off in anticipation of shabbas, and when he talked in the fading daylight, his mouth didn't seem to move. He and Cosmo were sipping beers.

Stephanie, a doctor, was in town from Minneapolis, where she was doing her residency in dermatology. She was slim and pretty, with a pale face, dark eyes and shoulder-length brown hair that she periodically tucked behind her ears. She was utterly un-made-up, and I instinctively imagined how she'd look in heels, mascara and a cocktail dress, something low-cut and flattering. She wore a buttercup-yellow turtleneck sweater that was just loose enough to be modest but which showed off her distinctly Midwestern figure, curvy and athletic.

"Let's let the ladies schmooze," Michael said, dragging Cosmo into the kitchen.

Once they'd gone, in quiet tones Stephanie explained that she and Michael had met on a Jewish Internet dating site called Frumster and that this was their second date ever, although they had been "corresponding for several months." They'd met for the first time in person over Halloween weekend, when Stephanie had come to New York for a visit. Michael had invited her over to cook shabbas dinner, but she'd declined. "I was going to go, but then I thought, 'This is a strange man. I can't just go to his apartment,'" she said. They borrowed a friend's place and had dinner there: neutral ground.

I asked her if she was Orthodox.

"I was raised Reform," she said. Like me.

"But you're becoming . . . more?"

"Well, I'm wearing jeans." She gestured toward her knees. "But, yes, I'm getting more into it."

Stephanie was what Michael called "traditional Reform," meaning she was raised in a lightly observant household but was gradually embracing custom. She was in town now for a month, doing a pediatric dermatology rotation at New York University Hospital. She was planning to attend classes at Machon Chana, a nearby Jewish women's school.

"They have a two-year program I'm thinking about doing," she whispered. "They say about half the women drop out by the end of the first year because they get married."

She giggled and asked if she could use my room to change.

"Sure," I said, imagining the horrors of Machon Chana,

and asked her to give me just a few seconds to tidy up. Once in my room, I performed a frantic sweep, as if the Drug Enforcement Agency were at the door. Anything potentially offensive or incriminating went into a bin on the far side of my bed. What was offensive? I had no idea. I erred on the side of caution, hiding birth control pills, underwear, rolling papers, copies of *Vogue*. I emerged after too many minutes.

"All yours!"

She came out in full shabbas getup, and for the first time, I found myself face-to-face with one of *those* women. Poor Stephanie, I thought. A doctor, and she's still been brainwashed by this nonsense.

She and Michael were attending different shabbas dinners, and he would be sleeping on our couch that night. He prepared by putting a sports coat over his black fleece and stringing a spare copy of our house keys on an elastic band, which he then stepped into and pulled up around his waist, like a belt. It is against Jewish law to carry anything on shabbas, and this is one of the infinite ways the Orthodox cheat the system: around the waist instead of in the pocket is A-OK with God.

THAT NIGHT, Cosmo had invited me to accompany him to shabbas dinner at the home of his friends, Shlomo and Hadassah Goldfarb, a prominent young married couple in the neighborhood. Shlomo, who was twenty-eight, was in the diamond business and ran a shop on Eastern Parkway called Gold

Jewelers. Hadassah, twenty-seven, was a homemaker, Shlomo's part-time secretary and, in Cosmo's estimation, "at least
the second-best cook in Crown Heights."

The *tsnius* conventions hold that all females over the age of
three should wear modest clothing. A married woman must
also cover her hair, so that no one but her husband sees it. Some
keep their hair but wear head scarves. I had one skirt that fell
below the knee, so that made it easy to choose what to wear.
Because a blizzard had just dumped ten inches of snow on New
York, I paired my long skirt with two sweaters and heavy boots.
It was the same switcheroo as Stephanie, going from modernity back to eighteenth-century Russia. The whole thing made
me feel itchy.

We were halfway there when Cosmo noticed I was carrying a handbag.

"A purse!" he exclaimed, pointing.

"What?"

"You cannot have a purse."

"Why not?"

"You can't *carry* anything."

I trudged back to the apartment and dropped it off, stuffing my coat pockets with wallet, keys and a cell phone set to
mute.

"You better not jingle," Cosmo said when I caught up with
him. "Have you taken everything jingly out?"

I told him I had.

Compared to Manhattan's cramped, crowded streets—
to the treeless tenements on the Lower East Side or even the

cookie-cutter brownstones on the Upper West—Crown Heights is open and spacious, virtually pioneer country. Legendary New York landscape architects Frederick Law Olmsted and Calvert Vaux, the men who built Central Park, designed the neighborhood's central artery, Eastern Parkway, as an old-style European boulevard. Towering elm trees line the wide street, the center of which has four lanes of traffic, two in either direction. Two wide brick pedestrian walkways flank the cars, and two more lanes of traffic flank those, meaning if your home is on Eastern Parkway, your neighbors across the street are a good fifty yards away. Which was a nice feature, especially during the holidays.

Ever since the 1991 Crown Heights Riots, spurred by a car accident in which a member of Rabbi Schneerson's motorcade swerved and killed a seven-year-old black child, the neighborhood has operated under a kind of forced racial harmony, uneasy but upheld by a heavy police presence. The accident occurred on President Street, about twenty paces from what is now the Goldfarb home, where we were going.

There are rarely violent flare-ups anymore, but the tensions play out in other ways. Cosmo and I navigated sloppy piles of snow and slush on the four blocks that separated our apartment from Shlomo and Hadassah's. Most of the houses in Crown Heights are brick, single-family homes set back from the street, with little porches and bay windows in their living rooms. Most are occupied by Lubavitchers, who have bought up the deeds to many neighborhood properties. The few houses occupied by black families all had elaborate Christmas decorations, flashing lights, giant trees in the windows or entire nativity scenes on their lawns. One apartment we passed had a whole speaker system lined up in the window, facing out, blasting Caribbean Christmas carols into the dark street below. This was the sound track playing as we walked to dinner.

The festive aggressions are hardly one-sided. Year-round, many Lubavitchers decorate their homes with yellow nylon flags embroidered with crowns and the words "Welcome, Moshiach!" Many keep cardboard signs in the windows reminding passersby that "He is coming!" The Goldfarbs didn't go in for all that stuff. The couple lived with their three children, all under the age of ten, in around nine hundred square feet on the second floor of a weatherworn brownstone. They kept their simple iron gate unlocked. A few scattered plastic toys peeked out of the heaps of snow on the lawn.

Deborah, who came up to my hip, greeted us at the door by shrieking "I have a fish tank!" and running upstairs. She was the oldest and went by Debbie. Debbie and her sister Yael, a head smaller than her sister, wore identical full-length dark purple velvet dresses with ruffles at the shoulders and long-sleeve gray T-shirts underneath. They had gotten a fish tank, but no fish yet, for Hanukkah. They had also gotten a board game called Zingo and a host of other toys, which Shlomo and Hadassah were rolling out slowly, even though the holiday had already ended, to make the joy of the season last. Debbie grabbed me by the hand and dragged me in to show me the lifeless tank, which had a plastic castle and building water inside, and which she could just barely reach on her tippy toes. It was up the stairs in the dining room, next to the giant bookshelves of leather-bound, gilded prayer books. A large portrait of Rabbi Schneerson hung in the hall and a more cinematic black-and-white photograph hung by the fish tank, showing the Grand Rebbe, surrounded by black-hatted admirers, raising a kiddush cup.

I had wanted to bring wine, but Cosmo said no. Jewish law forbids carrying anything on shabbas, so we would have had to bring it over earlier in the day. When we arrived, the table, set for sixteen, was already half-full. Shlomo, handsome and stoic, sat at the head. Tan and boyish, with a full brow and a thick head of black hair, he wore a black yarmulke, wool trousers and a tan V-neck merino wool sweater from J.Crew that Hadassah bought him a year ago, but which he'd only started wearing recently. She went over at one point to flip back the collar and show me the tag. He had a small paunch, the result of a weakness for junk food.

To Shlomo's left was his friend Ezra, dark-haired and fat, who neither spoke nor ate. To Ezra's left was another friend, Gil, fair-haired and fatter, who had two helpings of everything. At the near end of the table was Dinah, one of Hadassah's sisters, who was slumped over a white plastic plate, eating vegetable sushi with her fingers. She wore Ugg boots, a long skirt and a poorly combed wig, and she held her face so close to the plate that she barely needed to rotate her wrist to move the cucumber rolls from table to mouth. Cosmo dropped his coat and hat on a couch in the sitting room, where a giant display of shabbas candles burned in ornate silver holders, and settled in next to Gil. He began to say kiddush, the blessing over the wine.

I said a quiet hello to the men, who nodded vaguely in my direction. Then I froze in the doorway, unsure of what to do. Should I sit? Should I make conversation? Normally under these circumstances, when surrounded by people I don't know, I sidle up to someone and peck away at them pleasantly, the way I learned at countless cocktail parties, asking strangers about themselves. But are the women in this community even allowed to ask questions of the men? Every course of action I considered seemed potentially fraught. On the way over, I'd told Cosmo I was nervous about making a mistake and offending everyone, and he'd said, "Don't be ridiculous. Just act like me." I looked over and he was standing at the table, eyes closed, chanting in Hebrew. I decided the best solution was to find Hadassah in the kitchen, introduce myself, and see if there was anything I could do to help.

When I found her, Hadassah was spooning giant heaps of Hellmann's mayonnaise into a large wooden bowl of iceberg lettuce.

"Welcome! Welcome!" she said when she saw me, dropping the spoon in the jar and enveloping me in a hug. Two kisses on the cheek, another hug, and we were ready to exchange names.

Cosmo had finished the prayer and come in behind me.

He nodded and went over to the sink, muttered a blessing under his breath, filled a carafe with cold water and dumped it on his hands, then motioned for me to do the same.

Hadassah returned to the mayonnaise and began her interrogation. Where was I from? What did I do? How did I like Crown Heights? There was hardly time to answer in between questions and autobiographical ephemera. She was from California, where her parents, now in their seventies, still ran a kosher restaurant in downtown Los Angeles. She and Shlomo had met eight years earlier, when they were introduced by his cousin, a friend of hers. They had married after a few months. "It's nice," she said. "You grow up together." She wore loose-fitting clothes, a black skirt, black shirt and black Puma ankle socks. Covering her head was a lovely, shimmering silk scarf, dyed in pinks and yellows and overlaid with gold. It was the only touch of color she allowed herself, but it was bright against her tan skin. She still had her hair but kept it hidden. A few tufts peaking out of the scarf revealed that despite her youth, Hadassah was going gray. She smiled easily and spoke with a barely audible lisp. She was half a foot shorter than I, with wide hips and soft, rounded shoulders. Hugging her felt like a trip back into some storybook childhood where all women wear soft cotton dresses and smell like chicken soup.

"What do you do?" she said.

I told her I wrote about fashion.

"I *love* fashion!" she squealed and dried her hands on her skirt. She shopped at Bloomingdale's, but her sister-in-law put her on a budget recently, so only the essentials. The kids each got one new outfit this fall for Rosh Hashanah, the Jewish New Year. She got a warm coat, a new long skirt and a new shirt, all black. She handed me the bowl of salad and nudged me back into the dining room.

The men were gossiping about some petty scandal at 770, but even as they took turns speaking, no one heard a word of it. All attention inevitably drew back to the children, who took turns screaming about wanting dessert and chasing each other around the house. Hadassah shuffled around, tending to the kids, bringing them the harps they'd made at school out of rubber bands and paper plates, drying their tears when the harps broke and quizzing them on this week's Torah portion, which had something to do with Joseph, the one with the dreamy coat. The table was covered in an ivory-colored cloth, stained with big drops of sauce and red wine. In addition to the salad, there were bowls of spicy lima beans, cold noodles with carrots and dill, potato salad, hummus and olives.

"This food is going to be much better than Thanksgiving," Cosmo said.

There was no communal prayer. Everyone made their own contact with the divine and then dove in. The room quieted down for a moment until young Yehude, Shlomo's son, commanded the spotlight. He had a full head of dark tight ringlets—not payess, since unlike other Hasidim, most Lubavitchers don't wear long sidelocks. The curls came down to his chin, and a wide, guilty smile cut through cheeks, which were soft and round like rising dough. He wore blue pajama bottoms and a shirt that said I Love Daddy! Yehude climbed up on a chair, caught his breath. Throwing a fist into the air and summoning all the strength of his little lungs, he shouted, "Get off my property!"

"Yehudeleh!" Shlomo yelled. Hadassah raced to get him down. "Yehudeleh, honey, don't fall! Come to *tata*."

Yehudeleh wasn't going anywhere. He threw both fists up in the air and jumped up and down in place.

"Put up your dukes!" he screamed. "Put up your dukes!"

"They've been watching *I Love Lucy*," Hadassah explained apologetically. The Goldfarbs didn't have a television in their house, but with twenty-one cousins scattered around the neighborhood, they found it difficult to keep a close enough eye. They sent the kids to an ultra-Orthodox school, where they studied religion in the morning and had secular lessons in the low-blood-sugar afternoon hours, but Hadassah worried that they weren't learning enough about real life. "Sometimes I'm afraid it's a little ghetto," she said, meaning Russia, not Compton. Although she did see nascent signs of worldliness. The other day, Debbie, who had been given the choice of one new doll for Hanukkah, had picked a little girl with black skin, kinky hair and traditional African garb. "All we can do is try to show them a little more of the world than we saw," Hadassah said.

The Goldfarbs casually managed the chaos of their home— singing songs, dishing out nondairy tofu-based ice cream, grabbing knives just moments before they were stabbed into young eyeballs—and evening passed easily into night. I sat in silence for the first few courses, terrified of saying or doing something in violation of the innumerable shabbas rules. At one point, Hadassah and I were in the kitchen together, and I asked if she was raised Lubavitch. She said yes, that her mother had become observant early in Hadassah's life and passed that on to her children. She told a story about her mother in her Reform days, just as she was becoming more interested in a traditional way of life—right about where Stephanie was at the time. The family always went to see movies on Friday nights. The first shabbas after her mother decided to become more observant, she had a traditional meal and then, per family tradition, went to the movies. Only this time she watched *The Ten Commandments*.

I chuckled, and Hadassah looked at me, disappointed.

"A Jewish movie!" she said, clapping her hands to her thighs.

I laughed louder and nodded enthusiastically. Satisfied, Hadassah handed me two plastic bowls of chicken soup, and we carried them back to the men. When we arrived, Shlomo was complaining that he was getting fat.

"That's because you don't eat anything all day and then you come home at seven and you eat the whole house," Hadassah said.

"Wait," interrupted Gil. "You don't make your husband lunch?"

Shlomo shook his head sadly.

"She doesn't make breakfast either," he said.

"I take care of three children, and I work for you part-time, and I have dinner on the table every night at seven fifteen,"

Hadassah said, cheerful but defiant. "You want lunch, you go marry someone in my mother's generation."

"But you're the woman," Gil sputtered. "That's what you do."

"I do enough, thank you," Hadassah said. She went to the kitchen and returned with enormous plates of chicken, rice and kugel. The men brought out a bottle of Smirnoff and took sips from clear plastic cups. A collegial midmeal buzz set in. They teased Shlomo for putting up with such a neglectful wife. He half listened to their nudzhing but spent most of the evening staring out the window at the street below, as his fellow Hasidim struggled through banks of snow. From that window, you could almost see the house Shlomo grew up in, at 880 Eastern Parkway. He knew the names of every person walking down the street and periodically told us about them, speculating on whose houses they were coming from or going to. Crown Heights was his living room—had been since childhood. The walls and lawns and banks of snow that separated house from house slipped away when he looked out at the sidewalk. He dreamed of moving to a warmer climate but almost certainly never would.

Here is a man who knows who he is, I thought, who can feel fairly certain about everything that will happen for the rest of his life. There will be births, deaths, a few surprises. But there will not be the persistent burden of choice. Hadassah will make dinner but not breakfast or lunch. More children would come, if it please God, or they wouldn't. It would be a busy, pious life—exhausting and restrictive but filled with tiny joys. He would not be plagued with doubts about his lifestyle choices because he had barely made lifestyle choices. Long before Shlomo Goldfarb was even born, most of his decisions had already been made for him. His lot was hard work and selflessness before his family and God. By the age of twenty-nine, he would single-handedly support four children, his wife, his two sisters, his sister-in-law and his parents, with no hope of ever quitting his job or retiring. These were heavy burdens, and he bore them with pride.

"He takes after his grandmother," Hadassah said, looking adoringly at her husband. "You should have seen her. We'd say, 'You have to buy new shoes, bubee.' And she'd say, 'Why buy shoes? I'm just going to die.'" Everyone laughed. "It's true! You walk around her house and there were names taped under everything, for who was going to get it when she died. Under the lamp, 'Yaysef.' Under the piano, 'Shlomo.'"

Gil told a story about his father, who had starved and sacrificed his entire life in the Ukraine to be able to move his family out. His parents had gone every weekend to the local market to sell off all their worldly possessions, had applied for visas in every country and, of all places, the United States came through.

"He gave up everything for my sis and me," he said. "And when we finally got over here, we couldn't even make him eat because he was so used to starving, he had no appetite anymore."

It was getting late. Hadassah went into the kitchen and returned with dessert and a copy of *People* magazine. She flipped open to a feature titled "Worst Beards of the Year," with side-by-side photos of celebrities who'd grown ungainly facial hair. I went to get my coat while the men studied the pictorial, comparing the actors' beards to their own. Cosmo, who'd been quiet for most of dinner, zeroed in on one, jabbing his finger into the magazine.

"You know," he said, "Brad Pitt does look like me!"

I walked Hadassah down the hall to say good night, and we ducked into the bedroom she shares with Shlomo. There were his-and-hers double beds with pink floral comforters, separated by a wide aisle. Pink carpeting covered the floor. White lacquer bedroom furniture hugged the wall. We could have been on the set of *I Love Lucy*. She opened a dresser drawer and pulled out two pieces of jewelry she and Shlomo had recently designed: a detailed gold bracelet with diamonds and a simple brushed gold ring. Both were beautiful. I told her so, and she gave me a hug.

Hadassah Goldfarb, six months older than I, was just another of the harried Hasidic women I saw every morning, dragging children through the streets. Her house was a screaming mess. There were toys everywhere. After just two hours there I had a migraine I was pretty sure would actually split my head in half. But from somewhere deep in the recesses of my brain—in the recesses of my *soul*, the Lubavitchers would tell me, since every inkling toward an observant life is attributed to *neshoma*, to the God-given force within—there came a strange feeling of envy amid all the easy pity I was accustomed to feeling. My body wanted to run away, to put on high heels and blast the ache out of my skull with loud music and whatever else. But then after that, I knew I'd be right back where I started, on the armchair opposite Cosmo, watching him smoke cigarettes and wondering where to go from here. Hadassah and Shlomo had none of that. Young and settled, confined and exhausted, they seemed freakishly content.

FULL OF HADASSAH'S HEAVY, greasy food, Cosmo and I trundled home. He was wearing a brand-new brown wool coat he'd bought the previous week at Century 21, a discount clothing store in Lower Manhattan. To pass the time, he fished for compliments.

"This coat fits nicely," he said.

I nodded.

"I'm *very* happy with it."

He also wore a brown felt hat that he'd bought a year earlier for one hundred dollars.

"It was worth it," he declared.

When we got home, I collapsed into one of the armchairs.

Cosmo got another beer and settled on the couch. "I have made a decision," he announced.

"Oh yeah?"

"I have decided to give myself the same advice I give everyone else."

"What's that?"

"Nothing begets nothing."

"What does that mean?"

"If you want to get something out, you have to put something in."

"And . . . what does *that* mean?"

"It means I have decided to take a little more control of my life."

"Wonderful!"

He nodded and began to roll a cigarette.

"So, do you have a plan?"

He nodded solemnly. "I'm thinking of shaving these," he said, rubbing his cheeks with the backs of his knuckles, indicating the side parts of his beard.

"You know, you really should try jujitsu," he said, flicking ashes out the window into the cement courtyard below. "I talked to the woman at the gym about you. I told her you're nervous to try it, and she said she'd spar with you any night you want for free."

There was no way to communicate just how unappealing the prospect was of commuting an hour to Bay Ridge to wrestle around with some strange woman, so instead I said, "Sure. I'll give it a try."

"It's made me strong," Cosmo said. "Not physically. Well, physically also, but more mentally. I realize all the things I was afraid of, I'm not afraid of anymore."

He put out his cigarette.

"So, do you have a plan?" I asked. "What about going to school?"

"I'm thinking I'm going to try to get into a band," he said.

"But what about the copy shop? Are you ever going to leave?"

"I'm not sure I want to make decisions like this," he said. "Maybe the best thing is to wait and have the decisions make themselves."

"That sounds like a *terrific* idea."

"You know, it doesn't necessarily guarantee happiness," he said, "being *proactive*." He pronounced it "pro active," as two separate words, like it was some junk science he was in the process of demolishing.

"You've been working there for *seven years*," I said.

"Don't rub it in," he said.

We sat in silence for a minute.

"You should make a plan," I said.

"I know," he replied. "I cannot expect a long-legged Harvard woman to just walk into my life. I have to go out and do something."

"Eh," I said. "Harvard women aren't that great."

"Yeah," he replied. "And long legs are overrated."

Journey to the Warm Reaches of My Jewish Soul

People don't talk about loneliness much in New York, even though it is by many accounts the loneliest place in the world. There are more single-person households here than anywhere else in the country, more people jammed together in high-rise apartments but parceled out in little cells inside. The days after my breakup, I walked around the city sobbing, and no one said a thing. Later in the year, wonderful things happened to me, and I walked around beaming, and still no one met my eyes. It wasn't a surprise—I never meet anyone's eyes in the city, never ask anyone who's crying on the subway what's wrong—but still, being in Manhattan felt increasingly unbearable that winter. As much as I'd always told myself I was fine on my own, I'd gotten soft. On bad days or good ones, I wanted someone to tell. On cold days or any days, really, I longed for human contact. And it was not there. Companionship is hardly a guaranteed cure—my loneliest moments happened while I was packed in a car as a kid with my parents or tucked into bed as an adult next to Chad—but companionship, like a good outfit, at least fixes the outside.

"Sometimes I just want someone to hug," I told Madeleine.

"Sometimes there's no one to hug," she said.

But there was someone to hug: Hadassah Goldfarb. And there were warm kitchens and people to talk to, even if I couldn't talk much about my actual life. You can't really explain the Boom Boom Room or *Sex and the City* or Isaac the twenty-two-year-old luxury-denim model to a twenty-five-year-old Hasidic woman with three children. But you can watch her mix the Hellmann's into the iceberg lettuce and pretend for a few hours that nothing else exists in the world. You can ruffle the curls on little Yehudeleh's head and feel the warmth of his scalp and get him a nondairy kosher brownie if he wants one.

Instead of finding excuses to avoid Crown Heights, I started lingering there. I got to work late because I was killing time at Judaica World, looking at light-up ballpoint pens with little floating Stars of David inside and tiny plaster of Paris yeshiva boys glued on top. I started turning down invitations to dinner parties in Manhattan on Friday nights in hopes of being invited to shabbas dinner. Just as Cosmo was licking his chops at the lure of secular life, I was retreating into the soft belly of Orthodoxy. When could he come with me to a party? he wanted to know. When were we going dancing with my friends? That busty girl at my office I told him about, the

babe from California—when, oh when, could they meet? I
had other thoughts. Where were we going for Purim? What
were our plans for the second night of Pesach? I didn't give a
damn about these holidays—could give only the most cur-
sory retelling of the fables behind them—I just wanted more
excuses to go hide in someone's crowded living room.

One frigid winter morning on a lark, I stopped by Machon
Chana, the Jewish women's school down the block, and picked
up a glossy brochure. It had a picture of an austere hotel lobby
with Danish-modern furniture and a glowing fireplace on the
front. It looked like a pamphlet for a boutique hotel in Nor-
way but it was actually for "Yeshivacation," a program for Jewish women who felt they weren't quite Jewish enough. I was
not one of these women. It was not God but something else
that tempted me. The name Yeshivacation was charmingly
awful: a clunky portmanteau of "yeshiva," or religious school,
and "vacation." Floating above the fireplace was a tantalizing
offer: "Take a trip to the warm reaches of your Jewish soul!"

Inside the brochure was a picture of a bottle of red wine and
two long-stemmed glasses, set out suggestively in front of a
roaring fire. "Do you feel a sense of emptiness, your soul stifled
by its involvement in mundane life?" the accompanying text
asked. "Is your soul yearning for spirituality, thirsting to bask
in the knowledge of your Jewish heritage? Warm up your soul
by immersing it in study! Fan the embers of your soul until
they burst forth in flame! Treat your soul to the gift of freedom
to soar freely and break through the limitations of this world!"

When I got to work, I wrote to the e-mail address printed on the back of the brochure. I introduced myself as a non-observant Jew who found herself inexplicably interested in what a program like this might have to offer. I sent this off under the subject line, "Too late to join Yeshivacation?"

I had no idea at the time, but the arrival of my e-mail in Adinah Moscowitz's in-box in the administrative office of Machon Chana set off something like a fire alarm in Crown Heights. A wayward Jewess was there! A gettable, retrievable, teachable Jew of marrying age was "interested in attending." My cell phone rang seconds after I hit send. Adinah introduced herself and thanked me for my query. No, as it happened, it was not too late to join Yeshivacation, *Baruch Hashem*, Blessed the Name. Could she just ask me a few questions about myself? Great.

The question she asked, over and over again, in the grand Jewish tradition of asking ad nauseam until everyone exhausts himself and goes to bed, was *Why?* Why was I interested in attending? Why had I moved to Crown Heights? Why had my family not been more involved in our synagogue in Pittsburgh? Why, why, why, and also who. Who was I living with? Who did I know? Who was I and who did I want to be? Adinah was blunt and unsparing. She did not hide her disappointment upon hearing that no, I did not say the morning prayers each day, nor did I have my own copy of the Tanakh. She was relieved to learn that I knew the Hebrew alphabet. She was more enthusiastic when I told her about my yearly fast on Yom Kippur, omitting that I did this mostly as a crash diet before Fashion Week. When she asked whom I lived with, I dissembled, mumbling about having just moved in and not knowing my roommate well, using gender neutral pronouns throughout. Something told me platonic cohabitation with a Hasidic rabbi would be a disqualifier for Yeshivacation, if not a reason to haul in the *tsnius* police.

At seven the following Monday morning, with a heavy snow pounding down from the sky, I reported for my first davening class at Yeshivacation. Adinah was in the front office. She took one look at my cropped hair and my white alpaca snow boots with bright red laces, which I'd bought for a ski trip the previous year, and quickly introduced me to a pretty young woman named Ruchel. Ruchel would be my tutor for the week because . . . *Wow*, did I need help. Petrified of doing something wrong, I asked twice before helping myself to a foam cup of Maxwell House coffee and nondairy creamer out in the hall. Ruchel ushered me into the classroom and handed me an annotated edition of *Tehillat Hashem*, a standard prayer book. She had long brown hair exactly the same color as her long corduroy skirt and wore a pale blue sweater that matched her eyes. She was an instructor and dormitory supervisor at Machon Chana. Kind and genuine, she said that yes, there was much I didn't know, but plenty of time to catch up. I told her I was a writer, that I was single and that I was twenty-seven years old.

At this last revelation, every head in the room snapped toward me. I looked up and found nine sets of pitying eyes fixed in my direction. *Twenty-seven years old and unmarried!*

I was an old maid. I looked at Ruchel, who nodded encouragingly in the direction of my borrowed prayer book. I clumsily read the first line of the *schacharit*, or morning prayers, silently cursing all the time I'd wasted terrorizing my teachers at St. Sinai. The class listened as I fumbled through an effort to thank God for restoring my soul to my body, a prayer they'd all said the moment they woke up that morning. *And she's illiterate!* It is a Hasidic woman's primary job to teach her children Judaism, to make sure they speak Hebrew and Yiddish, that they say all the proper prayers at the proper times. Until you've mastered the fundamentals—something Lubavitchers achieve by the age of sixteen or so, after a lifelong intensive religious education—you cannot hope to marry. Who in God's name would want you?

"Don't worry," said Ilana, a heavyset eighteen-year-old goth Hasid, who wore earrings in the shape of gambling dice and chipped black polish on her nails. She came up next to me during break and clapped a friendly hand on my back. "You'll get it."

Up at the Boom Boom Room, twenty-seven was young and single a good thing. But down here at Machon Chana, I was a full-grown woman who had wasted ten of her childbearing years—doing what? They didn't want to know. All was forgiven; let's just turn to page three of *Tehillat Hashem,* please, and try to take fewer than twenty minutes sounding out the Hebrew this time. I had never thought of myself as old before, or even particularly as "aging," though my peers were already getting their first shots of Botox and beginning to fret about finding someone to marry. But now there were all these young girls looking at me like I was all washed up. It was an odd feeling. I had come here expecting to pity them—did pity them, pitied them every day when I bopped down Eastern Parkway to the subway that would take me out of Menachem Mendel's territory and into Tina Brown's. It made me sad to think that they would never have the feeling of absolute freedom and limitless possibility that I felt on my best days. It made them sad to think I would never be a sixty-year-old woman with twelve children and three dozen grandchildren wreaking havoc around me all the time. When I looked at them, I saw girls who would have only one first kiss in their entire lives; who would never read *Anna Karenina*, let alone have a passionate love affair; would never know the satisfaction of a great day at work followed by a late night blowing through someone else's cocaine. They looked at me and saw someone who very well might end up old and alone.

The schedule was jam-packed with seminars and activities, the vast majority of which I skipped for work. The first day was light—a tour of Crown Heights and a challah-baking workshop—but each day thereafter was a rigorous exploration of a major theme in Jewish life. Day three was devoted to "Love and Marriage—Hasidic Style." Day four was a fast. (The Jewish calendar includes lots of fast days, and this happened to be one.) Day six had a number of panels on the subject of kashruth, or the laws of kosher living, including "*Toiveling* Dishes, a Hands-on Demonstration" and an evening talk, given by the kind but decrepit Rabbi Garelik, called Moshiach—Why

the Urgency?" The highlight of the week, and the unmistak-
able apotheosis of the teachings of Yeshivacation, came on the
eighth night, when they took all the happy girls in the flower
of their youth (and the one strange, dim twenty-seven-year-
old) to a real live Hasidic wedding.

My week at Yeshivacation was a logistical nightmare. I
attended morning davening class, worked a full day, then
returned after dark for the evening program. This required me
to leap back and forth across the vast sartorial gulf that separated Crown Heights and Chelsea. Every day, I slid into some
horrible, dowdy amalgamation of every long item of clothing
I had, terrified someone would catch me looking like polyga-
mist cult leader Warren Jeffs's sixth wife. Arriving at work, I
tiptoed into the ladies' room and changed into my usual work
outfit, something short and tailored and black. Evenings
brought a scramble back into *tsnius*. Because I was too vain to
do this at the office, I changed in a dark corner on Eastern
Parkway, in an alcove between houses. This process involved
hiking a long skirt up on my waist and shimmying out of my
secular clothes. In place of heels came flats. In place of bare
legs came knee socks. I was just like Clark Kent, shedding the
spectacles that disguised him as a journalist. Only instead of
Superman, I became frumpy. Any Hasids passing by surely
thought I was deranged.

In this fashion, Manhattan life meshed awkwardly with
my newly deep engagement in Crown Heights. On the one
hand, there was Anya, the young married mother of three
who once confessed to me she couldn't remember her own

age. (We sat down with a piece of paper and figured it out: She was twenty-five.) On the other hand was a weeklong work project I undertook at the behest of my boss: "Stars Who Age Backward," a gallery and essay identifying celebrities who looked younger going into 2010 than they had at the turn of the millennium. One day I wrote a tribute to Alexander McQueen's Armadillo heels: twelve-inch claw-shaped python-covered hooves that retailed for $12,000. Another day I went to a Chinese auction, where Hasids bid on hand-painted portraits of Menachem Mendel Schneerson and listened quizzically as popular Jewish comedian and writer Joel Chasnoff told jokes about such topics as basketball, which fell far outside the typical Lubavitch woman's frame of reference. Women in Manhattan cheered on Elin Nordegren for her graceful divorce. Girls in Crown Heights dreamed of purple velvet wedding gowns with lace trim at the wrists. One afternoon at work, when I was supposed to be researching a profile of Molly Ringwald, I found myself transfixed by an obituary for Yitta Schwartz, a Hungarian émigré and member of the Satmar Hasidim. Yitta, who had survived the Bergen-Belsen concentration camp, left a progeny of two thousand—children, grandchildren, great- and great-great-grandchildren—when she died at the age of ninety-three. The *Times* memorialized her under the headline "God Said Multiply, and Did She Ever."

This whiplash reached an apex on the final night of Yeshivacation. We had learned about mikvahs. We had eaten jelly candies while a shorn mother-daughter pair talked about shopping for wigs and convincing agnostic husbands of the

importance of a kosher kitchen. Now, at the teleological con-
clusion of all our training, we were ready for the big show: a
wedding. My outfit for the evening was a long black skirt
with a red and blue plaid shirt tucked in. Plaid was having a
nice moment in fashion, and I usually wore this top unbut-
toned in what came to be called the "off-duty model style,"
with a pair of jeans and flat ankle boots. I wore the ankle
boots that night with a pair of green wool ski socks pulled up
under the hem of my skirt. I looked like a homeless hipster,
like I'd taken an extra-potent hit of mescaline and wandered
out of Williamsburg, picking up articles of clothing out of
garbage cans and putting them on along the way.

I walked into the wedding and was shocked to see a parade
of couture. The women were dressed gorgeously, their hair
and makeup done to perfection. I recognized designer gowns:
Versace, Gucci, Vera Wang. As they danced, holding hands
and kicking up their feet in one large turning circle, I saw the
red soles of a dozen Louboutins. Half the noses in the room
were identical ski slopes, with a straight bridge and small
round nostrils—certainly not the noses they were born with.
I was shocked! I was mortified. I looked down at my ridiculous homeless hipster outfit and felt the urge to run away.

Before I could, the impeccably dressed women at the wedding grabbed my hands and pulled me into a large circle dancing around the bride. I danced next to Danya, a student from
Berkeley and, of all the students at Yeshivacation, the one closest to my age and disposition. She wore jeans and some sort of

knee-length hippie apron. Chana, the bride, was dressed head to toe in white lace. A high white fence separated her from Yitzhak, her new husband, and also kept the enormous men's and women's gatherings distinct. The marriage had taken place at 770 earlier in the day, and the party was in a giant event space across the street, which hosted around five Hasidic weddings a week. As the Yeshivacation girls filed past the men's area, I peeked through the door and, for as long as they let me, watched the dense mass of formally dressed Hasids, wearing black top hats and black suits, dancing in a circle, hoisting the groom and his father and uncles up in chairs. A Hasidic band played onstage. A long cord traced along the back of the room and connected to one large speaker in the women's section, which blasted the same music to a much different scene.

As the night went on, and we just kept spinning in circles, I began to forget how inappropriately I was dressed, forget even what a weird old biddy I was to everyone there. I locked arms with Danya and a middle-aged married Hasidic woman next to me, wearing a lavender dress and a smooth brown wig. We kicked our legs and twisted side to side while the band on the men's section pumped out chorus after chorus of Jewish wedding music. Chana, the young bride, red-faced and beaming, stood in the middle, turning small circles of her own. Her hair—it looked like it was still her own, not yet shorn or covered by a scarf—fell in long brown ringlets, which bounced as she danced. Her makeup was perfect, and her eyes were full of happy tears. Periodically, on some prompting—I couldn't tell what—all the women, arms linked, rushed in on her, closing ranks, cinching tight, and she waved her hands like a beauty queen.

Hasidic Jews believe a woman is closer to God on her wedding day. She has special prayers she gets to say and these get more traction with the Divine. At one point, Chana reached out and grabbed me from the circle. I had no idea what was happening and dug in my heels, shaking my head, urging her to find someone else, but she insisted. She held my hands in hers and we twirled around, just the two of us, while she spoke a prayer in Hebrew. I searched my body for any feeling of holiness, for anything at all. My thoughts immediately skipped forward a few hours, to the room where Chana and her betrothed would spend their first night together—almost certainly the first time either would touch the bare flesh of a member of the opposite sex. As she whispered in Hebrew, I looked at her closed eyes. She opened her eyes, smiled peacefully and let go of my hands as the circle of women closed around her.

Could this possibly be happiness?

A Stick with
Two Ends

Hasidim do not date as the rest of us do, going out to dinner, telling the same three or four well-polished stories designed to emphasize our charm and humor, and then going back to someone's apartment and groping each other in the dark. Hasidim date aggressively, with intent to marry, like darling Chana, who as I write this is probably already a mother of two. Marriages like hers occurred all the time in my neighborhood, and they were broadcast in red on a scrolling neon sign posted above the House of Glatt. Cosmo was a learned scholar and therefore a catch. Although he had decided he wasn't Jewish anymore, he hadn't told anyone, so members of the community continued to try to find him a match. Occasionally Hadassah Goldfarb would foist him on some poor Hasidische soul, even though he tried to beg off. But because Hadassah was such a great cook, he'd oblige.

During my first week living in the apartment, Cosmo went

out on a date with a twenty-three-year-old Lubavitcher woman named Varda. He'd dreaded it from the start, and she'd confirmed his worst expectations. She was young and naïve. He took her to Park Slope, to a fancy coffee shop, and she asked him questions like, "Is Vienna in Austria or is Austria in Vienna?" She was timid and withdrawn. "In these modern times, a woman needs to have a projecting manner," he told me as we sat in the living room after the fact.

"Oh, but she's just a kid," I said.

"In my world, people at twenty-three are real people," he replied.

"Was she pretty at least? What did she look like?"

"Do you know Kelsey Grammer?"

I did know Kelsey Grammer, actually. I'd recently spent some time with the television actor and his blond, buxom, soon-to-be ex-wife at their sprawling Bridgehampton estate for a magazine story I'd written. I told Cosmo about this. "You could be from Mars for that price!" he howled. Grammer was one of his favorite actors. He made me describe the house in painstaking detail: the size of the swimming pool out back, the dimensions and contents of the library, the texture of the zebra pelt the Grammers use as a rug in their solarium, what a solarium was. Poor Varda had reminded Cosmo of the *Frasier* actor because of her gap-toothed smile. She was doomed.

"There have been only two women I've ever *really* loved," Cosmo said. "One was married. She turned out to be less than I thought. Let's just say our attraction was purely physical."

The other was Odette.

"There is a kind of love where everything is just—it's right," he said. "You love and are loved in return. And that was her."

He met Odette while he was training to be a rabbi in South Africa. At the synagogue there, he taught a class in *Tanya*, the central Lubavitch text, and Odette's mother was one of his students.

"What did Odette look like?" I asked.

"She was a big girl. There was something about her . . . the cleavage."

He paused for laughter.

"She was smart, well educated, a big talker—blah, blah, blah. I love that. We dated for a month. She dumped me. I felt miserable, and I talked her into dating me again for another month."

It didn't work out. Before long, rabbinical school ended and he was back in the United States. Odette went on to marry some other guy.

Falling in love accounted for about 24 percent of Cosmo's 25 percent chance at a radically different life. My escapist dreams tended more toward the geographical, but wherever I went in my head, I took for granted that there would be a rugged stranger, possibly foreign, an excellent dancer who admired my eyes. Love, like religion or low-carb dieting, is an easy fix-all fantasy, the most alluring because it really can be true. There is nothing better than loving someone, not even being loved back. Love makes you forget about your pointless job or the fact that you're just now tipping over from the glory years of "tremendous potential" into the long slow era of squandering it. Love obliterates productivity; it turns virtue to vice. It can make even the simplest, stupidest interactions seem bottomless in their profundity. When I'm in love, I can spend what seem at the time to be extremely productive hours reading and rereading a single e-mail.

Someone once told me that every time you relive a memory you change it in small but irrevocable ways. So the more times you flash back to that one thing he said or that time you took a long drive on a spring afternoon when the forsythia was just blooming, the more the moment evolves in your mind. To me, this is the sweet magic of love, that no time is static, nothing is fixed. It doesn't begin in one place and go from there. Instead the whole sprawling mess of it shifts and changes over time, so the story of the forsythia writes and rewrites itself over and over, as does every moment before and after, smoothing and refining itself in a larger context, shading and coloring all the little corners of memory until your whole life is something softer: a photocopy of a photocopy of the original. First we write love stories, then they write us.

Love turns a lonely childhood into a series of small heartbreaks, little pops on violin strings that led me to you. Love turns a meandering career marked by strange detours and failures of ambition into a beeline straight into your arms. After losing his wife, the protagonist of Vladimir Nabokov's *Bend Sinister* longs to "immobilize" millions of moments in their life together, as if pulling the emergency brake on a train. What else would you cling to when you're stuck at a photocopy shop, or stuck wherever, but the promise of love? Not just to reset your life going forward but also to reach back in time, grab your childhood self by one little hand and say, "See, you're okay."

It is hard for me to mark the spot where hope bleeds into faith, but for Cosmo and me, in the winter of our discontent, love was not just something we wanted but something we believed in. In our own ways, we each felt we needed this thing that was invisible and intangible and seemingly impossible, and we needed it so much—we felt it was so central to our plans for self-redemption—that we had no choice but to have faith it would come. The love Cosmo wanted was a girlfriend, preferably a shiksa with a nice rack. The love I wanted was different, and not just because it didn't have tits. Exactly how it was different was hard for me to grasp exactly, like trying to hold a fistful of sand. It had something to do with Yitzhak and Emily Blunt, and something to do with Harold Bloom, and something to do with Chana on her wedding day. What I wanted to do was to draw a circle around people and call them "home."

IN THE FIRST WEEK of the New Year, Hadassah set Cosmo up on a shidduch date with a very sweet twenty-five-year-old Lubavitcher woman named Davinah, eligible in every way but unmarried, perhaps on account of a gender imbalance that was unsettling the foundations of domestic life in the

Lubavitch community. Secular America was deep in the throes of its own marriage crisis during this period, as young women for the first time in history were out-enrolling men in college and out-earning them in the workforce. "All the Single Ladies," an *Atlantic* magazine cover story, delved into the broad consequences of a dwindling population of quality men. In the Lubavitch community, different as it was, the situation was much the same. Marriage rates were falling, dating customs were changing and the number of educated single women in their twenties was ticking up, up, up. Out in the secular world, the marriage rate among members of my generation was around 22 percent, down 7 percentage points from a decade earlier, according to a Pew survey that incited a frenzy. In Crown Heights, the reaction was no less dire, though the numbers were slightly different. A 2009 survey of 5,319 female high school graduates, all between the ages of 24 and 29, found that 735 remained unmarried—"a tragic 14 percent," according to the authors of the survey, called the NASI project. "I just feel there are more 'better' girls than 'better' boys," a matchmaker named Raizy Edelman told *Shmais*, a Crown Heights community newspaper, as part of their special investigation into the neighborhood's "shidduch crisis." Many attributed the problem to a growing population. Because the Lubavitch community procreates at such a rapid clip, its numbers increase dramatically year to year. That means there are considerably more eighteen-year-olds, both male and female, this year than there were, say, five years ago. The problem for women like Davinah, according to this theory, is that her male peers are choosing to marry younger women. This wouldn't be a problem if there were older men for her to date and marry, but they were all taken. Or mostly taken. There was still Cosmo.

Davinah was an accountant from California. Kind, pretty, *frum*—the gamut. By all accounts, she was an extremely eligible candidate to become Mrs. Cosmo, mother of eight or nine ginger-haired babes. They made a date to meet one evening at a coffee shop in Park Slope.

"It was doomed from the start," Cosmo said the following night.

"Were you nervous?"

"I don't get stage fright."

"What happened?"

"What happened? I charmed the hell out of her."

Here's what happened: Cosmo had arrived at the coffee shop to find lovely, devout Davinah, in modest dress, patiently awaiting him. She had been told she was going out with a brilliant, charismatic, thirty-year-old rabbi—a scholar, a mensch. In fact, she had been set up with a shabbas-flouting heretic: a rebel, an agnostic, a former pillar of his community who was in the process of having the Yid knocked out of him by jujitsu and the promise of citizenship. He was Adam minutes after the apple. After engaging her in a heated two-hour debate about religion, he tore off his yarmulke and told her there is no God.

"I think the problems started when I ordered half-and-half in my coffee."

"I . . . don't think so."

After that they went to a bookstore. Hasidim are supposed to steer clear of secular culture. They are not supposed to read non-Jewish books, see non-Jewish movies or page through the collected poems of W. H. Auden in the back corner of a Barnes & Noble. For a Lubavitcher woman wandering around a giant Western media emporium, cold, hard facts were the safest bet, so Davinah delicately made her way to the history section.

"She wanted to read books about the American Revolution," Cosmo said, slumping his shoulders and hanging his head. "She likes people in uniform: Grant, Washington. Meanwhile my eyes were like *this big*"—he stretched his hands wide. "I went straight for Auden, then Dante."

Cosmo sat on the floor, reading Dante's *Inferno*, while Davinah hovered in the periphery. She was terrified. She was turned on. He barely noticed.

"I can't shake the feeling that this girl who worked in the bookstore was flirting with me," he said, "which is completely inappropriate."

The next morning Davinah sent him a text message apologizing for being "really judgmental sounding" and expressing hope that "you do find G-d." She didn't want to see him again, she said, and the reason was "you are the kind of guy a girl slowly falls in love with." She signed off adorably, "I hope I don't sound like an idiot. ;)"

"Maybe she just likes bad boys," he said.

The night after his date, Cosmo came as my guest to a

film premiere at the Time Warner Center in Columbus Circle, opposite the southwest corner of Central Park. The movie starred Claire Danes as an autistic cattle whisperer, whose specialty was designing slaughterhouses. Cosmo missed the screening of the film because he couldn't get out of work in time, but he made it for the dinner party afterward, held at a swanky Italian restaurant downstairs.

The Time Warner Center is the glass slipper of shopping malls, encased in crystal, with sweeping views of the park. During the day, you can stand in the back window of the J.Crew store and look out over the treetops to tourists in horse-drawn carriages and taxicabs shuttling harried business-people to and from their usual three-course lunches. Outside the enormous semicircular entry, it smells like Manhattan concentrate: a combination of gasoline, soot, perfume, hot dogs, sewer wafts and horse manure. Inside, it smells like new cashmere sweaters, floor wax, Italian leather shoes still in their boxes, buttery croissants from the bakery on the third floor. There are restaurants in the mall that serve five-hundred-dollar sushi lunches, stores that sell three-thousand-dollar diamond pavé evening bags and a hotel that hoists you forty stories up into some of the most expensive air in the world. In any of these places, including the J.Crew, which sells the same clothes for the same prices as every other J.Crew in America, you can press your forehead against a window and fog up a patch of the New York skyline. For the rich, who never have to come down, Manhattan is a collection of floating worlds like this, a big crystal jungle gym suspended in the clouds. Even before September 11, it was hard for me to look at these buildings without feeling a desperate urge to ride to the top and without also imagining them shattering to the ground. The Time Warner Center is what Zeus would step on if he ever married a Jewish girl.

That night's party, like most parties in New York, was thrown by a miniature ageless doyenne named Peggy Siegal. Peggy was an institution in the city, a party planner for the glamorous and well-heeled. She wore doll-size Chanel suits, ballet flats, and an assortment of perfectly smooth, perfectly coiffed wigs. On the occasion of her sixtieth birthday, she published online a complete list of all her doctors, including the plastic surgeon who "gave [her] a new neck." Her parties were lavish affairs, filled with celebrities, socialites and a small collection of preapproved journalists, invited only for our ability to enhance any of the other attendees'—although preferably the host's—public profile, bank accounts and fame. Peggy always smiled ecstatically when I arrived at her events. After years of inviting me to her parties, she seemed to have no idea of my name.

Dinner that evening was rigatoni followed by half a roast chicken, carrots and mashed potatoes, with piled-high communal plates of buffalo mozzarella and prosciutto to start and chocolate truffles, cake and ice cream for dessert. Cosmo, dressed in his best suit, arrived early and wandered around the mall, passing time until the screening wrapped up. I met him at the door to the restaurant, handed him his ticket and led him right to the bar for a vodka shot to calm his nerves.

I persuaded him to tell the story of his date with Davinah and for fifteen minutes he held a crowd of agents and film executives captive. He finished the story with a flourish, took his seat at a table opposite half the cast of *The Sopranos* and demolished an entire plate of prosciutto.

"Next time I'm not dressing up for a date," he said when we got back to Brooklyn that night, still discussing poor Davinah. It was around one in the morning, and we both sat in the kitchen, waiting for the kettle to boil.

"What did you wear?"

Cosmo sighed, blowing a lungful of cigarette smoke out the window.

"My colorful pants."

I imagined Cosmo strutting through Park Slope in his amazing Technicolor dream pants. I had never seen this particular garment before but somehow the image made sense: Cosmo in Skittles trousers. Cosmo dressed up like the handicapped bathroom stall at the *Daily Beast*. Cosmo riding a rainbow straight to hell.

"And my orange socks," he added.

"It's nice to dress up for a date," I said.

"We have a Russian expression: It's a stick that has two ends."

"In America, we say it's a double-edged sword."

"The Russian expression is better."

The kettle whistled, and Cosmo did nothing.

"She was really smart, Davinah," he said. "Really well spoken. She talks a mile a minute. I like that." Cosmo's type.

"She sounds pretty great, actually. Especially considering what you put her through. Maybe you should give her a chance?"

"She wasn't well educated, though. That bothers me."

"But that's not her fault. You're never going to find a Hasidic girl in Crown Heights who's 'well educated.' What matters is that she's smart, right?"

He was suddenly fully absorbed in the making of tea.

NOT THAT I was really one to talk. I was dating occasionally, which is to say facing down the prospect of dying alone several nights a week over artisanal pizza and "How about a bottle of . . . the Pinot Noir?" The prospect of dating for the first time in years was exciting and exhausting in equal measure. Generally speaking, I like dates. I especially like the awkward parts, the nerves, the special strangeness of a first meeting, accidentally kissing someone on the ear instead of the cheek. I like losing my balance on unfamiliar pavement in high heels, and the rush of uncertainty before I recover, when I almost stumble or sometimes do stumble, and it's still okay. I like anything strange for the momentary rush of it, for the little pinpricks on your skin that let you know you're alive.

But mostly I went on these dates because of a lack of imagination, a gravitational pull back to my old dreamed-of life. I'd taken this weird, dreary detour to Crown Heights. But in a way that's the whole point of a life lived in deferment. You suffer a setback, and as quickly as possible, you get up, you dust yourself off and you begin clawing your way back toward the original distant, unreachable goal. Man, apartment, job, Manhattan—the whole movie, nothing left out. The girl I had spent my whole life wanting to be wanted *that*, and so the girl I was pursued it, even though all these dates left me pretty much cold. There were things I needed in this initial period—mostly I sought, and got, reassurance that I was "pretty enough"—but beyond that, I was a closed system, untouchable in every way but the most superficial. Every night, I'd put on these showstopping outfits, and I'd look in the mirror and think, "Fine."

I went out with Isaac, the model from Salt Lake City. I went out with Ben the filmmaker, who once wrote an entire scene in a major motion picture about his own penis. I went out with John, an attorney. I went out with Frank, who loved monsters. Frank and I shared a bottle of Pinot Noir in his bachelor pad, with its parquet floors and dearth of furniture or paper products. I barely took a sip. A few hours later, while Frank was still sleeping, the depth of unfeeling in my gut suddenly took on its own sense of urgency. I made a break for the door, knocking over my full glass of wine, sending it shattering to the ground. In the absence of paper towels and with a mortal fear of turning on the lights, I grabbed the lone sponge in the sink and did my best to sop up the mess before racing out without leaving a note.

"Did you kill someone on your way out this morning?" Frank e-mailed to ask.

"I'm worried about what this looks like ten years from

now," my colleague Jacob said when I arrived at work seemingly splattered in blood.

"This"—he waved a hand up and down, roughly in my direction—"does not go on forever."

"This" culminated in a trip to the symphony one winter night with my friend Steven and his girlfriend, plus two other couples. Steven arranged my blind date for the night far in advance. Unbeknownst to me, the setup was with a man named David, a bald, five-foot-tall film producer who happened to be dating my friend Frances. When I learned this, my one thought was: Of course. The universe does not send us signs. We are not in dialogue with the universe, but if we were, at this point I would have thrown a glass of water in its face and marched out.

On the night of the symphony, David bailed, and I was left to shuffle alone through Carnegie Hall in my highest heels, surrounded by happy couples holding hands. As I dragged myself to my seat, I passed Steven and rolled my eyes. "Please kill me," I whispered. He took my elbow and pulled me into a row of orchestra seats.

"You journalists, all you do is wait for things to *happen*, and then when they do, you just want to run and hide."

Steven is in public relations.

"This is a nightmare," I said.

"So what," he said. "Lean into it."

"Excuse me?"

"Lean into it."

Lean into it. What the hell kind of advice is that? It's easy to say if you're a happy, wealthy, forty-year-old public relations bigwig with a gorgeous, talented girlfriend who is about to become your fiancée. It's a lot easier to *lean into* a charmed life in a four-story brownstone on the Upper West Side than it is to lean into an hour and a half of Mahler's Second when you are hopelessly alone in the world, when your night will end with an hour-long solitary subway ride and twenty minutes rapping to yourself in the pouring rain while pit bulls bark at you from a dented van. Leaning into that is like leaning into a fist.

"Lean into it," he said, and I rolled my eyes again and walked past.

I sunk down in my seat and surveyed Carnegie Hall, which was drafty. Old people up way past their bedtimes doddered to and fro. In the movie version of my life, the man of my dreams would have been sitting somewhere in that auditorium at that moment. And just when I was feeling lowest, when I was lost and hopeless and alone, he would catch my eye and smile. He would pull me close just by looking at me, and for the first time ever, my smooth tall cylinder with no parts for joining would melt and soften into him. We wouldn't even have to talk, maybe. He would have kind eyes and a big soul and I would know instantly that he was mine. The train would slow to a halt on its tracks. Time would curl in around us. Everything else would slip away.

Why can't life just be like a movie sometimes? Why can't

the prince come and carry us off to happily ever after—even just once?

I sat stiffly for an hour and twenty minutes, while the conductor led his symphony through Mahler's Second, which is also called "Resurrection." After that I went to dinner with friends at a restaurant on the Bowery and picked up our waiter, leaving him my business card with the check. He texted the next week to see if I wanted to go out, but I was leaning into a shabbas dinner by then and never bothered to reply.

The Outer Reaches
of the Universe

In his short story "Monte Sant'Angelo," Arthur Miller describes the whole of Jewish history as "packing bundles and getting away." If you're a Jew in New York in the media business, and this ancient stirring rises up within you, by far the easiest place to go is Los Angeles. It's like New York, only worse and with more cars.

It wasn't until I boarded a seven a.m. flight to Los Angeles on the last day of the month that I realized I'd completely missed my five-year anniversary in New York, the point at which, according to the inviolable gospel of Candace Bushnell, I officially became a New Yorker. It was a milestone I'd eagerly anticipated since childhood, since long before I first landed in town, all saucer eyed and chubby. I swallowed a sliver of Ambien on the plane and thought back to how I'd inadvertently celebrated my anniversary: dancing at a subterranean nightclub with some model friends and the trust fund artist who paid for their drugs.

California beckoned, and the Ambien started to kick in. I drifted off to the opening scenes of *Inglourious Basterds,* soothed by the slaughter of Nazis. I woke on the West Coast, a new promised land. It was a whole sixty degrees outside, and while the plane taxied, I worked through the logistics of a cross-country move. How long does it take to become a Californian?

The trip was only five days. I was meeting my friend Lucy there, and we were staying at a borrowed mansion in the Hollywood Hills, the barely used property of her family friends, a prominent entertainment industry couple. The house was on Hollywood Boulevard, atop a long driveway so steep we sang to our rental car as we floored it up the slope: "Go, go, Volvo, *go!*" I slept in the master bedroom, in a bed that may as well have been a cloud, with white Italian cotton sheets and a skylight that spanned almost the entire ceiling. A large Jacuzzi jutted out from the eastern side of the two-story home, and every morning I sat naked in the tub, watching the low pink sun rise over downtown LA. There were Emmys everywhere, on virtually every surface. And Writers Guild awards and Screen Actors Guild awards and books lovingly autographed by old, dear friends, like T. Coraghessan Boyle. Angelina, the housekeeper, came every other day, even though the actual owners of the place hadn't been home for months.

Los Angeles has always felt to me like a giant studio lot and all the people there merely extras, happy to make union rates to stroll around in the background of one another's lives. Crawling through traffic in someone else's car, sleeping like death in someone else's bed, visiting places I have mostly seen before on-screen—it feels more like scratching a path through celluloid than moving around in a three-dimensional world. Mulholland Drive was F. Scott Fitzgerald's before it was David Hockney's before it was Jack Nicholson's (and by extension Roman Polanski's and thirteen-year-old Samantha Geimer's) before it was David Lynch's before it was mine. On my first day in town, I wound my way up Mulholland to visit a screenwriter friend beside her pool, where we ate pudding cups and drank champagne from a sixty-four-ounce bottle of Cristal she'd received as a gift from a producer. She had just completed three days of rewrites on a film called *Hot Tub Time Machine*. This is life in Los Angeles, or a certain kind of life at least: writing and rewriting other people's stories, then drinking from novelty bottles of champagne beside your enormous rented kidney-shaped pool.

Lucy and I had come out for a few reasons. It was the Grammys, so there were parties. They were more or less the same parties you could get in New York; the biggest difference was that here, you had to drive to them. We were going to an opening at the Hammer Museum in Westwood of a renowned artist who drew doorknobs on graph paper using Bic pens and Wite-Out. We were going to spend a day in Malibu. We wanted to see the famous sculpture of Herakles at the Getty Villa, the one in which the Roman hero is depicted in full splendor, dangling a hard-won lion's pelt at his side—the

Platonic ideal of masculinity, save his missing penis, snapped off by vandals.

We were also there to work. Lucy is a screenwriter and playwright, and she was interviewing for staff jobs on television shows. She has blond hair and big dancing blue eyes and is without question the most captivating person I know. She gestures wildly and feels deeply, and the way she pulls you into her bubble is to spin you up in a story of insanity or outrage, as if knitting you into a sweater. Lucy's job is to tell stories but she could also lead armies if she wanted to, such is her gift for dramatic tension. She is also, not incidentally, an actor.

I was reporting out of our Los Angeles bureau for a few days. The bureau, which we called *Beast West*, and which was less a bureau than six cubicles in a West Hollywood office building, was a magical coven of brilliance, run by a pin-thin South African woman named Gabé. Gabé had begun her career as Tina's secretary at *Tatler*, following her to *Vanity Fair* and *Talk*. They were soul mates. Tina called Gabé "Gabs" and Gabé called Tina "Teen." Gabé drinks white wine spritzers, wears this-season Marc Jacobs and, in a good mood, will tell stories from the set of *Zoolander*, which she helped make. Mother only to a rescue dog named Snoopy (female), she became mother to all of us, in a fashion, sending me sweaters in the mail and giving life advice. We had traveled to Doha together, and the night of my breakup, she was the one I'd called. When, months later, I was still sulking around the office, my dyed-brown hair shoved under a knit cap, Tina suggested I move to Los Angeles to get a change of scenery. I asked to stay in New York and she said I could, "provided you go blond again."

I did not go blond again, but I did go to LA. Gabé took me for drinks at Bar Marmont. A year later, once the *Beast* had merged with *Newsweek* magazine, we would spend a lot more time together, once memorably raising Princess Diana from the dead for a story that ran when the late princess would have been fifty years old. We spent a week then trapped in a kind of séance, imagining what Diana would have worn, who she would have slept with, what kinds of things she might tweet about were she still alive. Without an ounce of makeup on her face and a social calendar scheduled entirely around piano lessons, Gabé was the most glamorous woman on the planet. She made outfitting a dead princess seem like a terribly chic and sensible thing to do. Her restorative abilities were miraculous; it was enough just to be in a room with her.

One of LA's very few virtues is that it's a breeding ground for strange things. This makes it a marvelous place to visit and a terrible place to live because chances are, if you stay more than a week, you'll end up in some sort of cult. I had come to Los Angeles mostly because I had learned of an up-and-coming faith healer who specialized in treating bankers, actors and professional athletes—people who seemingly had everything but still weren't happy. His clients included anyone who could pay the $300 to $500 he charged for an hour-and-a-half session, conducted in the converted garage behind his Santa Monica home. I'd heard his method involved choking his clients until they nearly lost consciousness and then pounding their chests while shouting about the subtle beauty of life. My appointment was for eight-thirty on Monday morning.

I arrived at my faith healer's home a full hour early and so went to have a coffee and peruse the bookshelf at the local Scientology reading room down the street. The wacko religious fringe is my favorite part of the West Coast, and any time I've gone, I've always tried to make time for at least one trip to the far reaches of the universe. I spent my extra hour that morning drinking a drip coffee with soy milk and paging through *Dianetics* by L. Ron Hubbard.

The faith healer was lurking behind a wooden gate that led to his backyard when I pulled up, a few minutes before our scheduled meeting time. I could tell it was him because he was six foot five and had shoulder-length gray hair and unblinking ice-blue eyes: the physique of an athlete, the physical presence of a sociopath. "Hello, Rebecca," he said in a deep, whisper-soft voice. Then he gave the heavy gate a tiny push so it creaked open, comically slowly. I expected a black cat to leap screaming out of the bushes and land, claws out, on my face. Instead, he calmly walked me down the short flagstone path and into his garage, where it was freezing from jacked-up air conditioning.

"You're cold," he said knowingly, as if he had just telepathically hooked himself up to my nervous system. He passed me a plush brown blanket that appeared to have been made out of teddy bear pelts and asked me to sit down on the couch.

I removed my sandals, plopped down cross-legged under the cover and surveyed the room. It was decorated in a style that might best be described as French Country Lunatic. Opposite the couch was a matching chair, in the same overstuffed shape and taupe fabric, as if they'd been bought as a pair at Jennifer Convertibles. Next to the chair, where he sat, was a life-size stuffed animal tiger—not a real tiger that had been prepared by a taxidermist but more like a Beanie Baby on steroids. Behind him was a wall covered top to bottom with a cornucopia of religious imagery: the Virgin Mary with delicate hands clasped around her glowing, anatomically correct heart, a Hubble-style rendering of the cosmos, Vishnu, Buddha, abstract pictures of Jesus and so on.

"So tell me, Rebecca," he said, "what brings you here today?"

"Well," I replied, "I wanted to write a profile of you for my day job, as a journalist, but your wife said you wouldn't do an interview, you would only do a 'session,' so here I am."

He nodded as if I'd just confessed to crack addiction and then explained to me that journalism was an elaborate ruse, that my brain had tricked me into coming to see him by telling me it was "work" because the truth was I needed him, and deep down my subconscious knew it.

"Okay," I said. He asked me to try my best to take this seriously. I said that I would and meant it.

He asked me about my life. I ran him through the gamut. He listened politely, as if he'd just seen this episode and already knew how it would end. When I finally stopped talking, he put his fingertips together in a pose of contemplation and brought them to his lips. "Do you mind if I come and lay hands on you?" he asked.

"Um," I replied. "No?"

He came over and sat down next to me on the couch, so close our thighs were touching. Placing one hand on my mid-back and the other on my collarbone, he explained that he was now going to remove a number of "energetic vampire energies" that were clinging to different parts of my body, like my lymph nodes and my heart. Here's what had happened, he explained: There had been so much loneliness in my childhood that at some point very early in my life, around the age of two or three, I had simply done what any sad little girl would have: I froze my true essence in my lumbar spine. Releasing those vampire energies—a process that would involve a pretty simple breathing exercise that would cause me to convulse and hyperventilate—would help free that little girl and set me on the path to happiness and success, once and for all. Professional athletes and Wall Street titans flew their private jets into California for the privilege of these sessions, and when they emerged, they hit home runs and made billions. The same would happen to me. He would perform a host of smaller miracles as well: I would no longer be cold all the time. I would shed what he called my "little girl voice." "When you get back to New York, you'll notice yourself sounding more and more like a woman."

It all sounded good to me, except the part about hyperventilating to the brink of unconsciousness, but what the hell, it would be nice not to have to carry a sweater around all the time. He set about identifying my vampire energies and having me address them diplomatically, which he said would set them free. One energy, which he labeled "Daddy's Little Girl," was attached to my stomach and had something to do with anger I felt toward my father. He had me beg my independence from "Daddy's Little Girl," then lean forward and take three loud, deep breaths. While I exhaled, he threw me backward against the couch. My eyelids fluttered and my shoulders shook. This happened five more times, while he rid me of "Prom Queen," "Girl Interrupted," and the rest of my demons, all of whom were named after romantic comedies or nail polish colors at any New York salon. I began crying from the emotional and physical strain of the whole endeavor about halfway through, when he had me speak to the spirits of all the siblings I'd wanted but never gotten, who apparently had a stranglehold on my liver.

Then we moved to a folding chair in the center of the garage. He went over to the stereo to put on a homemade CD called *Five Elements of Love: Awaken Your Immortal Body Through Inner Smile Meditation.* I know that's the name because he gave me a copy to take home with me at the end of our session. It has a collage of images from his wall on the front, and the title is spelled out in clip-art letters that look like they were cut from magazines, as if for a kidnapper's ransom note. As we began the final purge, of toddler Rebecca from my lower back, the music came on. It sounded like his voice singing, slow and melodic, the same lyric over and over: "This is your second chance." To complement the sound track, he sat next to me speak-singing the line in a much deeper voice, a few seconds before the recording, to create a spooky echoing effect. *THE TIME FOR YOUR REDEMPTION IS NOW NOW NOW.* If I'd had enough oxygen going to my brain, I probably would have laughed. We repeated the procedure of deep breathing followed by flinging me back against the chair until I was scared I was actually going to die and began begging him to stop. "If this is your time, this is your time," he said and repeated the cycle just once more. Once I'd regained my breath, we hugged and he left the room, handing me a red envelope on the way out. I had been instructed by his wife to leave cash for the session at my discretion.

His wife called to check on me a few days later, and then again a few days after that. I was more or less cured, she said, and would just require occasional visits with the faith healer for upkeep. She got my e-mail address and sent me a Paperless Post invitation for a session a month later, when he was making a tour through New York to accommodate his East Coast clients, but I declined. At first the whole thing seemed harmless and funny to me, just another kooky thing rich people did when it turned out money didn't cure all their problems. But the more distance I got from my faith healing, the more it grated on my nerves. It wasn't just that the whole thing was exploitative and ridiculous—promising to solve people's deepest troubles with $500 worth of near strangulation—but also that it cut off the possibility of external solutions. It was anti-emotion deodorant, a little girl wishing for God on an eyelash. It was a story to tell yourself instead of the truth, an action to take in place of real action. I thought about Menachem Mendel Schneerson and the crying bit from *Likkutei Sichot*: "When a person destroys his own inner Temple, no amount of weeping [or, presumably, hyperventilating] can ever rebuild it. Instead, he should perform actual deeds, for 'one positive action is worth a thousand sighs.'" After the third invitation for a checkup, I left them a message, using the most womanly voice I could muster, asking them to please remove me from their mailing list. (They did not.)

THE CHARMS OF Los Angeles self-destruct after seventy-two hours. It's just too spread out, too shiny, new and distant feeling, especially when you're used to being jostled around for most of the day. New York is lonely because of the sheer human density of the place, because you can get right up against people and still be by yourself. Los Angeles is just lonely. Everyone's in his own airtight bubble, shouting into cell phone headsets, picking their noses behind the tinted windows of their SUVs. In New York, when things happen, at least you hear them. Police cars whiz down Ninth Avenue. Couples scream at each other on the street. Once I was in Los Angeles working on a story for the *Wall Street Journal*, and in my hotel, on my floor, former Democratic vice presidential candidate John Edwards snuck in to visit his mistress Rielle Hunter and their love child. He even had a kerfuffle with a *National Enquirer* reporter in the hallway, but I heard none of it. I was tucked away in my noiseproof room, watching a marathon of *The Real Housewives of Atlanta*.

I took the red-eye back to New York the next night and was so eager to get on the plane, I arrived at the airport two hours before my flight and planted myself in a sticky booth at Malibu Al's Beach Bar. Two piña coladas and half a Valium later, I was ready for takeoff. The flight was almost empty. While we taxied, I arranged myself along a block of three seats, cocooned in cheap felt airline blankets, a mask covering my eyes. Just as I began to drift off, I heard the two men sitting opposite each other in front of me discover a personal connection: They were both en route to Haiti, which had just been leveled by an earthquake that had killed up to three thousand people and left much of the population homeless. One of the men was a freelance photojournalist, going to document the destruction. The other was an aid worker, going to help. They talked through the entire flight about what they expected to do and see. "Shut up, shut up, shut up," I thought, trying and failing to get to sleep. In the movie version of my life, I would rouse myself from my half-drugged slumber and join the conversation at this point. When we landed, I would quit my job and follow them south to document the suffering, which while not necessarily helping tremendously, at least would be better than writing about shoes. Instead I took a Town Car back to Brooklyn, slept fitfully till nine a.m., and made my way back into work.

Finding God

I f God to you is youth and beauty, well—here He is: ten or twelve or fourteen sixteen-year-old girls in stilettos and fetal lamb fur (or combat boots and silk chiffon, or a large feather headpiece and flesh-toned underwear, or absolutely anything at all), floating down a white strip toward a wall of flashing bulbs.

God in this form descends on New York twice a year, for eight days of presentations, parties and swanning around in elaborate hats for whoever might be looking. Fashion Week is an exquisite circus, a trade show for the world's prettiest people and things. Its animating spirit is envy. It is an entire world governed by the belief that the right dress can change everything. These people were my people. I loved every moment and prayed for it to end quickly.

The hot topic on the first morning of Fashion Week was a supposedly boiling feud between half the senior members of the fashion press and a thirteen-year-old Chicago-based fashion blogger named Tavi Gevinson. In Paris, the previous week, pint-size Tavi, who wrote under the name Style Rookie, had worn a large pink bow on her head while sitting in the front row of the Christian Dior show. She was photographed by an editor for Italian fashion magazine *Grazia*, who was sitting behind her and found her view partially obscured by Tavi's headpiece. This led to considerable consternation in the audience of the shows—a distress that was swapped out within a few hours of the start of the week by the news that designer Alexander McQueen, a fashion titan, had hanged himself.

There is always a scandal or a tragedy in fashion, just as there is always someone to hate or cry over in global politics or middle school, and that's part of what makes it fun. Fashion is a closed universe contained within a very open one. We all wear clothes, and to varying degrees we all care about what we put on our bodies. But only a very small number of us particularly care if Christian Lacroix is going bankrupt or gap-toothed models were hot this season or what the impact will be of a python shortage in Florida. Fashion people care very much about these things, and also about other fashion people. Just as you can identify your favorite athlete, I can point out my favorite market editor from fifty yards away, and I can also tell you who made her dress. I've never taken a sip of Guinness, but I can list a dozen pairs of shoes in socialite Daphne Guinness's collection, and I know where her boyfriend, public intellectual and bon vivant Bernard-Henri Lévi, buys his shirts.

Most of the sane world will think this is insipid, but I have always loved fashion people. They know how to live.

That February, a new advertising campaign cropped up in the New York City subway system. Almost no one involved in the fashion business noticed because almost no one in fashion takes the subway, but I did—an hour each way, back and forth from Crown Heights. The advertising campaign was sponsored by the Times Square Church, a house of worship built during the 1980s crack epidemic. It featured a rainbow-colored word collage set against a simple white background. In the center of the collage was a question: "What is God?" Surrounding it was a few dozen stabs at definition. God is "a father." God is "the one with your answer." God is "powerful," "merciful," "able to protect." God is "the one who loves you." God is "there when no one else is." As I rode from Brooklyn to the city every morning, and back every night, I read through all the things God was and then played a round or two of the game myself. God is . . . a huge admirer of your work. God thinks you look *great* today. God sees all the sacrifices you're making and your innermost desires and your greatest fears, and God wants you to know that it's all going to work out beautifully in the end.

A foot of snow fell on New York in the twenty-four hours before the start of Fashion Week, just as Tavi was making her way to town and McQueen was tightening the noose. I went with my friend Maria to the openings of two new nightclubs on the evening the blizzard hit, as the first few inches floated down from the sky. We drank champagne cocktails next to a small, wedge-shaped indoor swimming pool, wistfully declining, like the rest of the fashion press in attendance, the half-cut cheeseburgers passed around by aspiring models on the waitstaff. We ate dinner at a nearby French restaurant, at a table next to Katie Holmes, who was dressed head to toe in Burberry and spent the evening nibbling around the edges of a croque monsieur. After she left, the waiter told us how nice she was, how "down-to-earth." We speculated viciously about the true cost of that croque monsieur, paid in sessions with a Scientology Center nutritionist. We ordered the poached skate and, at the last minute, a burger and fries.

For the last time that February, Fashion Week was headquartered in adjoining giant white party tents constructed over Manhattan's Bryant Park, just a block away from the Times Square Church. The Tents, as they were called, were guarded by bouncers, blocked off by metal gates and surrounded by photographers and hired girls handing out leaflets and copies of the daily trades. Inevitably, the People for the Ethical Treatment of Animals would show up for an afternoon or two, to protest *Vogue* editor Anna Wintour's reliably opulent furs or the occasional egregious collection, made from fur harvested from fetal lambs skinned while they were still in the womb, or some other new and luxurious atrocity everyone was dying to wear.

It took me five years to learn the truth about Fashion Week, which is that it is a complete slapdash mess and, apart from the big-time fashion editors and tween celebrities paid to populate the front rows, no one knows anything. Anyone in a giant pair of sunglasses who affects a haughty enough attitude can breeze right in and probably get a decent seat. The trick is unwavering confidence. On the first morning, a blazing, cornea-searing glare refracted in all directions off the newly fallen snow, so I wore my biggest pair of ten-dollar sunglasses while traversing the single block between the subway and the Tents. When I walked in, pecking away at my Black-Berry, two wire service photographers without the faintest idea who I was dropped to their knees to take my picture. A camera crew from Japan rushed over and a woman tried to interview me about my shoes. I focused on not tripping and falling. I had no idea who these people were, but Fashion Week is an assembly line of these interactions. People are constantly discovering each other, only to discover someone better nearby. I spent a few seconds talking to the Japanese television host, not knowing if the camera was even on, and then I took off my sunglasses. It dawned on the film crew that I was no one, and the scrum of photographers and the Japanese television host just walked away, midsentence.

Inside, the Tents were rimmed with sponsor booths, where aspiring models handed out Balance bars and McDonald's coffee, directed you to the AOL media lounge or invited you to check out the Home Shopping Network display. No one at Fashion Week would be caught dead eating any of these products or visiting any of these booths, so the effect is a centripetal crush in the main tent, with women in towering heels and flamboyant outfits trying to avoid contact with any of the heathen advertisers who make the whole thing possible. Only the coolest and the least cool attendees venture to the outer realm—the people who have no reason to care.

People begin lining up a half hour before shows are scheduled to start, forming a crowd in front of a few twenty-two-year-old publicists propped up behind a card table with lists of seating assignments. The war in Iraq was a triumph of planning and preparation compared to the average preshow mania. At some point, when at least some of the several hundred attendees have received their seating assignments, the doors will open and everyone will stream in, making their way to their or someone else's small white padded wooden folding chair. At the back wall, at the head of the runway, which is covered in protective plastic, a swarm of photographers will have already taken their positions. As the attendees filter in, everyone checks everyone else out, scans faces for fame or recognition and constructs a mental hierarchy of the place. Every show is an instantaneously self-generating school cafeteria— you take your seat, you see who's sitting next to you, maybe you say hello but probably not. Twenty to thirty minutes later, a black-clad publicist talking frantically into a headset pulls the plastic sheeting off the runway. The din falls to a murmur, the lights dim, the music explodes out of the speaker system. A series of spotlights illuminate the runway, a heavenly beam cutting through clouds. In this moment, fashion edges toward religion. The models are so close and the crowd is so quiet. The bass line of the music is so heavy you feel it in your bones.

Three or four minutes later, it's over. The lights come on. We pack and leave. Maybe there is a swag bag—a scented candle, two lipsticks, a recycled brown paper notebook with the name of the designer embossed on an organic wood pencil tucked into the binding—or maybe not. Maybe you see someone you vaguely recognize or someone you met the other night or your oldest friend, and in that case you go kiss her on the cheek and spend a minute discussing how "really of the moment" the collection was or how "derivative" and when was the last time the designer actually had a new idea? You ogle Tavi and observe a moment of silence for McQueen and make a vow you never follow up on, to have lunch as soon as the "madness ends."

I wanted to bring Hadassah Goldfarb, fashion lover, to a show or party sometime that week. I was desperate to make it work, but the constraints of raising three children and observing a severely restrictive set of religious obligations made scheduling difficult. Fashion Week really gets going right around the time most women in Crown Heights are throwing the first braided loaves of shabbas challah in the oven. Most shows take place in the hours when mothers are driving their children to and from Beis Chaya Mushka and the rest of the Crown Heights yeshivas. Parties start around eleven at night.

Fashion people haul all sorts of accessories and entourages with them to the shows, and sometimes this baggage is accidentally mistaken for fashion itself. At the end of Fashion Week in February, the *Wall Street Journal* ran a clever

front-page story about how the hot accessory this year was
children—actual children, squirming in their front-row seats,
leaving trails of cookie crumbs on the runways and scuttling
around backstage with chocolate-smeared fingers, talking
about playing dress-up with the models. I wondered what
would happen if Hadassah came along and the photographers
took to it, and suddenly black hats were the new black. And
then I discovered that in 1993, Jean Paul Gaultier's fall collection was inspired by the ultra-Orthodox and featured an
assortment of *tsnius*-appropriate pieces, presented in a Paris
showroom while a fiddler played traditional Jewish music. For
the presentation, known as "Rabbi Chic," models wore
Mohawks and sidelocks. Menorahs lined the walls. The invitations were lettered in Hebraic-style script and the attendees,
many of them Jewish department store executives, were served
Manischewitz wine. The collection was a smash. After the
show, Ellin Saltzman, fashion director of Bergdorf Goodman,
told the *New York Times*, "As a Jewish-American princess, I
wasn't offended at all. I just cut through all that Judaic stuff
and looked at the clothes. Underneath that was a very commercial collection." Hadassah Goldfarb was *so* 1993.

The nineties, of course, were a more innocent time. In
2011, Christian Dior creative director John Galliano got
knackered at a French café and went on an anti-Semitic tirade
that turned the entire fashion business, save Kate Moss, into
crusading Zionists (or at least enthusiastic and diplomatic
defenders of Jews). It lasted about six months.

The first collection I saw was by Richard Chai. It paired

flowing pastel chiffon gowns with heavy gray Timberland boots. One critic described it as "the broody-quirky harnessing of nineties grunge." It looked like what Winona Ryder would have worn out to her mailbox during one of the more difficult stages of her life. It too was a very commercial collection. I wrote an enthusiastic fifty-word review. Then I went home to Crown Heights.

COSMO E-MAILED LATER that week, as I was waiting for the Phillip Lim show to start. There was no subject line and the text read, in entirety:

> hey!
> i have some good news!
> we should celebrate!

I was busy coveting British It Girl Alexa Chung's outfit, which she was modeling in the front row, but took a moment to write back. What was the good news?

> my papers came!!!
> in a few months i can file for green card!!!!

I wouldn't have been more shocked and excited if Cosmo had told me the Messiah Himself was riding a donkey down Eastern Parkway. Cosmo was finally going to be an American! He could leave the copy shop, leave Crown Heights, go anywhere he wanted and do anything. I wrote back, upping the exclamation-point ante, asking how he wanted to celebrate?!!?!!!!!!! We came up with a plan: cheeseburgers and *Avatar*.

The following night, I blew off seven fashion parties to eat *treyf* at the Burger Joint, a dingy soda shop in the back corner of Le Parker Meridien, one of the nicest hotels in New York, with my rabbi roommate. Cosmo ordered a cheeseburger with the works and a Coke, then took off the bun and shook out at least a teaspoon of salt on the cheesy, greasy patty, topped already with mayonnaise and ketchup, before taking a bite. This was his first-ever cheeseburger, and he seemed to consume the entire thing whole. I was two bites in when Cosmo leaped up to get back into the half-hour-long line to order a second burger. While he was in line, a nice young couple sidled up and asked if they could share the booth, since there was no place else to sit. They had just come from a cut-paper exhibit at the Museum of Arts and Design and were clearly on a third or fourth date. Sure, I said, then pointed out Cosmo, telling them we were out celebrating that his papers had come through and he would finally get a green card, after seven years of waiting. He returned with his burger to a small round of applause.

"What are you going to do?" I asked as he wolfed down the second cheeseburger.

"I think maybe I'll go to Brazil," he said.

"Yeah, but are you going to leave the copy shop?"

"I'll cross that bridge when I come to it."

"But you're nearly there."

He stopped eating his burger and fries and shot me a look that said, You're raining on my parade. I abandoned the nagging and switched to a line of questioning focused on new jujitsu moves he had learned and cute girls he'd encountered on the subway lately. He had recently moved up to the advanced jujitsu class and expanded his repertoire to Thai boxing.

He told me he'd had a nice conversation the other day with the head of his jujitsu school, a man everyone called Professor Grey, whom Cosmo worshipped. Professor Grey had said something that shook my roommate to the core. What he told the students in his advanced class was: "It's never going to get easier. You think you're getting your ass kicked now? It's only going to get worse. You think once you've mastered this set of moves you're home free? Wrong. The way things are now, with sweaty men throwing you to the ground, knocking you around, beating you senseless—that's the best it's ever going to get."

It put a momentary damper on the green card *treyf* fest. Why keep fighting if the fight only got harder, no matter what direction you took? An American citizen weighed down by a pound of beef and cheese didn't necessarily have a much clearer shot at happiness than the long-suffering, half-legal Russian immigrant. Then again: This was the easiest it was ever going to be! Might as well enjoy it.

We made our way uptown to the Lincoln Square Cinemas

for the nine-thirty showing of *Avatar* in 3-D. The movie had been out for months already, but the theater was packed, and though we were early, the best we could do were off-center seats a few rows too close to the screen. It was almost a three-hour movie, so we took turns going to the bathroom, then settled in and put on our special glasses. "I think I'll get a motorcycle license," Cosmo said. And after a few minutes: "Maybe I'll move to Harlem." He would become an EMT, or maybe an earth scientist and move to Texas and look for oil. He would get Denim Fajita back together and they would play some gigs. A whole new universe of possibilities spilled out before him as we sat in our 3-D glasses, waiting for the movie to start.

I looked over and saw Cosmo grinning ear to ear.

"Welcome to America, dude," I said.

THE FIRST THING Cosmo did with his newfound freedom was go to see Kim, my hairstylist, at her buttercup-colored salon on the Lower East Side. When he walked in, his hair was shaggy, his beard about six inches long. Like most Lubavitchers, he did not wear the traditional sidelocks, or payess, that other ultra-Orthodox men sport, but he did take a Samsonian view of his mane.

"Have you ever thought of shaving your beard?" I once asked him.

"Stylistically, without a beard, I would look like such a fuckface" was his reply.

Kim is five foot one, with a round face and big eyes. She dyes her hair light brown, in the fashion of many stylish Japanese women, and weaves strands of glitter in it to look festive. She wears a flowered dress and brown Christian Louboutin stiletto ankle boots, and because she also styles runway shows, she has fabulous stories about supermodels: who's sweet and who's a giant hungry bitch.

Kim took a matter-of-fact approach to both hair and love. She celebrated her birthdays—and all holidays—with a trip to see Hunkamania, a roving male strip revue. Her boyfriend was a prominent fashion photographer. They lived together downtown, along with Kim's morbidly obese cat, whom she always referred to as "my big kitty." Together, we had been through a lot, Kim and me: I came to her brunette with hair down to my shoulder blades, rail-straight thanks to a $300 "Japanese" treatment I underwent in Queens. She cut my first bob, which became my first pixie, and when I got bored of that, she bleached it to the whitest possible shade of blond. She took me back to brown after my breakup and then began layering in reds that winter. I liked making big changes to my hair for the same reason I liked the fashion business and New York: because it was a shortcut to reinvention. You can completely change the way you look, act, feel—at least for a few weeks— just by going blond. Hair may seem like a trivial underpinning for your identity, but it's not nothing. In some ultra-Orthodox communities, you have long, flowing brown hair and are a little girl one day, and then the next you are bald, a wife.

As part of every haircut, Kim gave her clients a little head massage.

I was not there to see it, but Kim reported a very productive session with Cosmo, once he recovered from the massage. He requested a full Mohawk and forbade her to even trim the beard, but she persuaded him to go with something a little more contemporary. The beard shrank down to three inches, the hair to more of a Caesar cut. In subsequent visits the beard would shrink more and more until Cosmo could have, and did, pass for any hipster in Bushwick.

The evening after his first haircut, Cosmo appeared in the doorway to my room, chomping away on dinner.

"What are you eating?" I asked.

"Bacon." I looked up and he was beaming as he chewed his gummy—wait, gummy?—meal.

"I don't remember you cooking bacon," I said. "And . . . it doesn't smell like bacon in here."

"I didn't cook it," he replied.

"So . . . you bought it cooked?"

"No."

I snapped my laptop closed on the bed. "Cosmo, are you eating raw bacon?"

"Yep!" he said. *Chew, chew, chew.*

"Oh God, no—" I spoke in my calmest worried-mama voice, but inside my stomach was already doing violence to dinner. "But . . . *trichinosis.*"

He hadn't cooked the bacon because he didn't want to *treyf* up his pans. He hadn't washed it because he didn't want to *treyf* up his sink. He was on the very brink of freedom, staring into the abyss but unwilling to cut the last threads. Once you cook bacon in a kosher kitchen, that's the end of it. The pans are ruined, the apartment is ruined, there are millions of invisible specks of bacon grease everywhere; a bacon pall is upon you.

"What if someone comes over for dinner?"

"When is the last time someone came over for dinner?"

Cosmo looked wounded, so I apologized. "Someone could totally come over for dinner," I said, doubting it as I surveyed the room. "Just cook the bacon next time, please, for your safety if nothing else."

"I don't do this to you," he said. "I don't tell you how to live your life."

"I'm not telling you how to live your life, I'm just saying that raw bacon can make you really sick."

We had an argument about this—him standing in the doorway defiantly gumming the bacon, me on my bed. I regretted the knee-jerk revulsion. In my defense, I am the child of *chemists*. We do not mess around with food-borne illness. But the argument quickly spun away from bacon and toward restrictions of any kind, to me telling Cosmo what he could and could not do. He didn't tell me what to eat, and I shouldn't tell him.

I was reading in the living room one night later that week when Cosmo trundled in after jujitsu looking particularly solemn. He stopped in the doorway.

"Everyone knows," he said.

"Everyone knows what?"

"I'm *frei*." He said this as if delivering a eulogy.

"What is *frei*?" I asked, worried he was in some kind of legal trouble, that his green card wasn't going to come through, that the *tsnius* police were about to come banging down our door.

"It means I'm free," Cosmo said. He flashed a rubber band smile, then went into the bathroom to wash his jujitsu uniform.

ON THE LAST NIGHT of Fashion Week, I went back to the apartment early and ran into my neighbor Chavie, who lived with her fiancé Chaim across the hall. They had both grown up in the Lubavitch community. Chavie had "done the whole all-girls-school thing" for a while, had even gotten as far as law school at NYU, but dropped out after her first year to become a trance DJ at local clubs. Chaim was "supposed to go to architecture school" but ended up "managing a pharmacy" in Crown Heights. They had been engaged for six and a half years. They were also heroin addicts.

When I ran into Chavie, she was scratching furiously at her wrists. "I need a cell phone," she said. This was the first time we'd met, and she only introduced herself later. I offered her mine, and she took it in to Chaim, climbing over the stacked armchairs that cluttered their entryway hall. She came back and joined me on the landing, smoking cigarettes and compulsively apologizing for it, even though it didn't bother me and I said so. She told me all about trance music, how it's "kind of a hippie scene," how "people there will just pass you a J. It's really nice. And they won't care if they ever see you again." She liked me because I looked "normal" and because I was wearing pants. She was petite and striking, with a slim angular face, heavy brows and giant chocolate-drop eyes. Her hair was pulled back in a haphazard ponytail and she wore loose-fitting cotton pants self-consciously. She explained that their phone and Internet had been turned off that morning, and that Chaim had a lot of "business calls" to make. Chaim had shoulder-length hair parted straight down the middle and dirty fingernails. He ducked into the hall after a few minutes, handed me back my BlackBerry and nodded his head once in thanks.

"Vogue," Chavie kept saying, looking at me, not acknowledging her fiancé's brief appearance. "Vogue, vogue, vogue," she said, and it dawned on me at last that this was a compliment.

"Thank you," I ventured.

She waved her cigarette around in the air and said, "You're welcome," then disappeared back into D6. "Come by anytime," she offered, "just knock."

I went in and buried myself under the covers, drifting off before ten to the muffled screams of our neighbors, possibly Chavie and Chaim, but I doubted it. Around two o'clock in the morning, I woke to the feeling of a hand delicately rustling my hair. The next sensation didn't cohere. It was a tiny thumping on the far side of my pillow, a little scamper across my bed. I opened my eyes just in time to catch the whip of a mouse's tail.

I leaped up and screamed long and loud but no one noticed, not the hollering neighbors, not Cosmo asleep in his bed, not Chavie, not Chaim, in their drug-induced haze. For the rest of the night I sat up with the lights on, curled up tight in a ball in the middle of my bed. The next day, I brought home a nuclear arsenal of rodenticide and scattered it around my room. I mentioned the mouse in a brief note to my mother, the scientist, and a plug-in sonar device arrived, without comment, a few days later in the mail. It was all useless. As soon as the lights went off, every sound was mice running around me—every rustle of wind, every muffled domestic dispute, every car passing on the street outside. I turned music on before I went to bed at night, singing along to Katy Perry like a mental patient until I eventually drifted off, only to wake again at the first little *scratch-scratch-scratch* on the floor.

California Gurls, we're unforgettable!
Daisy Dukes, bikinis on top!

On the final night of Fashion Week, I met my friend Rachel at the Boom Boom Room and we sat on a banquette eating miniature cheeseburgers. Rachel covered fashion and luxury goods for the *Wall Street Journal*. She has a dry and wicked sense of humor, and a worldview that holds that basically everyone is insane. "I'm surrounded by idiots" is a thing she often says. Rachel is one of the most loving people I've ever met. The way she shows love is by looking at you skeptically for thirty seconds and then shattering every illusion you ever had about life.

At Booms that night, I told her about my mouse problem and the fact that I would almost certainly die alone and also that I was increasingly finding my work to be something short of wholly satisfying. She looked at me, took a bite of a cheeseburger and said, "I don't want to hear anything more about this."

"Excuse me?" I said.

"You're on a spiritual journey," she said. "I don't want to hear about mice or men or any of this other crap."

"I'm on a spiritual what now?"

Rachel is not the world's most religious person. She is the daughter of a famous dentist and a powerhouse financial services executive. Her sister is a performance artist who once posed for a photographer dangling a blue-paint-soaked tampon in front of her crotch, while sitting naked and spread-eagle on a toilet. ("The Blue Period." Get it?)

"You've moved to Crown Heights and surrounded yourself with these maniacs for a reason," she said. "What do you think, this just happened?"

We are not in dialogue with the universe, I explained. The universe does not send us signs.

"Just figure it out," she said, and then she gave me a hug and a kiss. Courtney Love stumbled through the door with her entourage and was making her way noisily to the fireplace. I said good-bye to Rachel and then went up to the roof, where I lit my cigarette off a girl next to me. I wanted to stay up there in the clouds all night. But I looked around at all the identical boys and girls, smoking and preening and feeling like nothing under their clothes. The bubble popped. The effects of the drug wore off.

THE COMEDOWN AFTER Fashion Week is soft. The traveling circus moves on to London and suddenly it seems there is nothing but time. I had a drink after work one night with my friend Davi, whom I hadn't seen much since college. He was going to graduate school out of town, so he called me up and suggested we have a beer. We met at a little French place near my office and caught up on each other's lives. Davi is a lot like Rachel—clearheaded, intolerant of fools—but unlike her, he is an Orthodox Jew, and the subject of his thesis was partial Jewish identity. We talked about *War and Peace*, which I had just suggested to Cosmo, who declared the book to be "about nothing" and then went rummaging through my collection for something better.

"It made me sad," I told Davi. "All these people just looking for something to live for. It's war or it's love or it's God or money. And it works for a time, and then it doesn't, and then they have to go find something else to devote their lives to, until that doesn't work, and on and on. It's pointless."

"I don't see it that way," Davi said. "For me, it seemed like people searching for—I guess you could call them 'communities of meaning.' And it wasn't so much that they were fighting or praying necessarily, but that they were part of this group of people, and that's what gave meaning to their lives."

It's funny to think of the chirping women of *Sex and the City* as a community of meaning, but that's what they were, gabbing brainlessly about their boyfriends and shoes. Same goes for the fashion crowd, who aren't exactly the people you'd imagine having Thanksgiving with, until you do. It's messy and difficult to shape a family out of bosses and colleagues, professors and fictional characters, girlfriends, boyfriends, mothers, fathers, Hasidic Jews. It was strange to ride the subway to Fashion Week and think about all those women in their crazy outfits as part of my community of meaning, but that's what they are. Every mini-cheeseburger or after-work drink is a spiritual journey. It's no different really from finding people to make money with or fight wars with or gather together with to pray.

What is God? Call him love, call him a father, call him whatever name you want. It's the calling that matters, not the response. God is never the thing that fulfills you. God is the name for the hole.

Rough Beasts

One Friday night, Cosmo invited me to accompany him to dinner at the home of his friends Shaina and Avraham: "It will not be as nice as the Goldfarbs, and the food will not be as good."

"Sounds great," I said.

Shaina was an Israeli-born massage therapist with olive skin and green eyes so dark they looked black in the dim light of their apartment. Avraham was thin, pale, American. He was a rabbi, like Cosmo. They met while studying together in South Africa, at the second-best Lubavitch rabbinical school in the world, Cosmo said. According to my roommate, Avraham was brilliant, the star pupil. He spoke the way a dancer danced, light and quick. He made large gestures and lingered on his s's, so the words took on a ringing quality, like live wires hanging in the air. Like Cosmo, Avraham didn't lead a congregation. He traveled around the country, inspecting restaurant kitchens and performing the rituals necessary to certify them as kosher. Shaina and Avraham had three children under five.

Their apartment smelled strongly of freshly baked challah. It stood in such contrast to the dry cold air outside that once we arrived after the long walk over, I had to keep reminding myself I was still awake. There may be no more perfect food than a braided challah straight from the oven, burnished brown on top, soft and dense underneath. It's no wonder Jews have a prayer just for this bread. It's the first thing I learned in Hebrew school, and in my head it's one long word—*baruch-atah-Adonai-Eloheinu-melech-ha'olam-hamotzee-lechem-min-ha'aretz*—chanted as quickly as possible, while staring at a torn-off hunk of bread cooling cruelly in your hand. Shaina was unloading three warm challah loaves on the dinner table just as we walked in the door.

Another couple, with three children of their own, was already at the table. Gittel and Solomon were twenty-five. They had grown up a few doors away from each other, married as teenagers and had the kids in rapid succession, one-two-three, as if racing to make a family before the bread cooled. Gittel was breast-feeding her baby on the couch when we walked in. She had a round, sweet baby face herself and looked no more than eighteen years old. She told the story of a recent trip to the pharmacy to buy formula. She brought along her oldest child, who was three and a half. The pharmacist asked if the little girl was her sister, and Gittel laughingly explained the situation, watching his jaw slacken. "He couldn't believe it!" she said, giggling.

Solomon was bellicose and fat. Before dinner, the children ran around the apartment screaming, Gittel nursed on the couch, Shaina carted plates of food in from the kitchen, Avraham gave me an impromptu lecture on that week's Torah portion and Solomon sat at the far edge of the table and did nothing, just shouted occasionally at whoever would listen. He read celebrity tabloid magazines and wanted to know about Tiger Woods, so I tentatively ventured bits of my reporting, feeling ashamed that I knew as much about it as I did. He asked me if I had ever heard of a Hasidic fashion designer and then before I could answer went off on a tear, half in Yiddish, about how the man was a *faygeleh*—gay. He could not get over Cosmo's and my living arrangement and kept asking questions about how it worked. I saw Cosmo shrinking in humiliation a few seats away. "Do you want to go?" Cosmo mouthed, and I shook my head, I was fine. Before he could respond, it was time for the *broches* (pronounced "bra-chas"): time to chant blessings and then eat.

Avraham went around with a bottle of kosher wine, and we all held up small, engraved silver cups, which he filled to the absolute brim—a tradition meant to give a feeling of abundance on shabbas. During the week you can skimp, especially if you're twenty-five years old with three children. But for one day, you fill your cup until it's overflowing. We said the *broche*: Blessed art thou, Lord our God, King of the Universe, who gives us the fruit of the vine. Amen—and everyone drained his glass.

We said the *broche* over the bread: Blessed art thou, Lord our God, King of the Universe . . . Amen. Shaina passed around the challah, and we each ripped off a hunk. It was warm like just-spun cotton candy, with buttery whirls of steam rising from the center. Everyone ate.

Everyone ate but little Chaya, Gittel's oldest, who didn't touch her bite-size morsel. Children under three are exempted from elements of observance—an infant girl can wear short sleeves and doesn't have to participate in services or say prayers—but Chaya was just old enough to be on the hook. She was standing right next to me, playing with plastic Hebrew alphabet blocks at a doll-size Fisher-Price kiddie table, and unlike the rest of us, who were hungry for dinner after a long week, she didn't want to eat. Solomon saw this and a flash of anger came into his eyes. He shoved his chair away from the dining table, sloshing wine onto the tablecloth. Grabbing little Chaya by the shoulders, he shouted, "Eat!" Bewildered and terrified, she clamped her mouth shut and shook her head. With his thick sausage fingers, Solomon pried her jaws open, forced the small piece of challah inside and then held her chin tight against her skull until she managed to chew and swallow. When he let go, she began wailing, her cheeks red, her face smeared with snot and tears. I watched all of this in silent awe, like it was a documentary on the Discovery Channel.

Gittel went over to calm her down, and Avraham pulled Solomon into the kitchen. "Be a good husband," he said.

Solomon went upstairs to put the other children to bed. When he returned he announced he was going out. He didn't say where and didn't say when he'd be home. Gittel begged him not to go, grabbing at the fringe of his tallit, but he took off, making a few loud jokes on the way out. He left silence in his wake. It cannot have been the first time he'd acted this way, but the others seemed extra-conscious now, since a stranger was there. Cosmo looked like he wanted to die. Gittel dusted herself off, put a babe back on a boob, and the night continued without further interruption. Before I left she asked if I'd like her to set me up on a shidduch date with one of Solomon's friends.

It is impossible to count, but rough estimates suggest that Brooklyn is home to hundreds of thousands of ultra-Orthodox Jews, including the Lubavitchers, the Satmars, the Bobovers, and the Breslevers. The Lubavitchers have their own ambulances, called Hatzolah, their own hospitals and their own local law enforcement, the Shomrim. One August night during the year I lived among the ultra-Orthodox in Brooklyn, two men calmly exited a white car on Driggs Avenue, shot a twenty-five-year-old Satmar Hasid named Burech Halberstam in the abdomen and then stood over his body, pointing and laughing. A month later, a black Orthodox Jew was shot a few blocks away by a gunman hanging out of a green Mazda. That fall, the Shomrim were given bulletproof vests.

Gruesome murders by roaming thugs are an expected if tragic part of life for a people who've been threatened with death for most of their history. This is not a community of people who are particularly surprised when someone shoots a Jew, then stands laughing over the body. On top of that, there is the political aspect. Nothing unifies the neighborhood and city law enforcement, whose elected bosses depend on Jewish money for their campaigns, like an old-fashioned hate crime. Schneerson and his contemporaries cultivated close relationships with elected officials, giving the Lubavitchers a prominent voice, as Jewish leaders go, in city and national affairs. In 2010, Lubavitch leader Rabbi Yehuda Krinsky was named the most influential rabbi in America by one survey, topping non-Hasidic rabbis who represented movements in the millions and who managed enormous endowments. It's easy to caricature the Lubavitchers for their makeshift outreach efforts— the hand-painted mitzvah tanks, the pedi-sukkahs, made of cheap plywood fencing and driven around by teenage Hasids on tricked-out bicycles each fall. But the truth is, the Lubavitchers are a sophisticated international force. The Chabad-Lubavitch organization raises around $1 billion a year, according to *The Rebbe's Army* by journalist Sue Fishkoff. That buys a lot of Chabad houses around the world, and it also buys a lot of friendly attention from higher offices, helping to ensure certain territories never become too hostile to the Jews.

There are established social, economic and political pathways for confronting threats from the outside world. It is within the Lubavitch community that protections become murky. There's a zero-tolerance policy for anti-Semitism in Crown Heights, but neither Jewish nor secular law meddles too much inside people's homes. Lubavitchers range from billionaires to extremely poor. Many use food stamps and live in cramped apartments. In many respects, Lubavitch Hasidism is a matriarchy. Ask any Lubavitcher woman out of earshot of any of the men, and she'll confess to wearing the pants, in many respects, in her household. They teach the children religion; they often manage the family finances and keep the community's businesses in order while the men study and pray all day. Every morning, every ultra-Orthodox man says an extra prayer thanking God for not making him a woman, and it's not hard to see why. Not only do many Hasidic women bear upward of six children in their lifetimes, but they are also subject to countless atavistic rules. Cosmo and I lived two blocks away from the Crown Heights mikvah, where women must go each month to purify themselves after menstruating. Cosmo told me a dedicated rabbi was on duty twenty-four hours a day to examine stains left in a woman's underwear. Only he might determine, based on the color of the stain, whether the woman was fit for sex.

In this climate, between the poverty and the institutionalized misogyny, domestic abuse is rarely reported and almost never publicly addressed. During my time in Crown Heights, I met many men who adored their wives, who were loving and deferential, and even in the poorest households, treated the women like queens. But I also met men like Solomon. And I heard stories about others: the fathers of six, eight, twelve, who went cruising for prostitutes in the poorest neighborhoods of Brooklyn. There is a strange feeling of lawlessness in Crown Heights, even as its residents are pinned down by so many rules. When so much is forbidden, it can be hard to distinguish one sin from another: a cheeseburger from a hooker from a slap across a child's face. And when the biggest threat has always come from the outside, I imagine it's hard to find the time or energy to look within. A year after I moved out, an eight-year-old boy named Leiby Kletzky was walking home from day camp when a neighbor named Levi Aron picked him up, brought him home, chopped him to pieces, wrapped up just his little feet and stored them in his freezer. It was reported later that the Shomrim had been tipped off that Aron was a wacko months before the crime, but they apparently never passed that information on to the police, who discovered little Leiby's remains after a frantic two-day search.

Gittel watched powerlessly as Solomon manhandled their child. After he left, she chuckled and moved on. Part of me wanted to grab her and her children and haul them out of there. Part of me wanted to run away myself. Instead, I did nothing. I ate my challah quietly and left before it got too late.

THE FOLLOWING rain-soaked weekend, I had to decline an invitation to shabbas with the Roths, another Crown Heights family, because all my earthly concerns were replaced by the "Women in the World: Stories and Solutions" summit, a conference sponsored by the *Daily Beast*. In typical Tina fashion, "Women in the World" was a lavish affair, drawing the boldest names from her Rolodex to the Hudson Theatre, in the Millennium Hotel in Times Square, for three days of programming focused on rape, "gendercide," and other things you wouldn't necessarily want to talk about over dinner. Few people can make rapid-fire panel discussions about institutionalized female infanticide feel both urgent and glamorous, but that was Tina's special skill. The guest list was impossibly tight and stringently (but politely) enforced. Hillary Clinton came. Madeleine Albright came. Meryl Streep not only came but also played a Northern Irish civil rights worker in a staged reading of a documentary play about abused women, directed by Julie Taymor, the woman who would later be fired from the Broadway production of *Spider-Man*.

Tina, in her blue power suits and perfectly frosted hair, presided regally over the conference, which so resembled her in taste and tone that it felt as if we had all gathered inside her frontal lobe. The schedule was jam-packed, with just enough time for clipped rounds of applause between panels before Tina would bound up onstage: "Wasn't she *mahhvelous*? And now we're going to hear from . . ." Katie Couric interviewed Queen Rania of Jordan about "the lives of girls." Diane Sawyer interviewed Marietou Diarra, a Senegalese woman, about female genital cutting. Barbara Walters, Tory Burch, Valerie Jarrett, Diane von Furstenberg, Donna Karan and on and on and on: They all came and talked and made sweet jokes about their hair or clothes by way of transition into the heavier issues of the day. They all milled around in pantsuits and modest heels. They all had the Chardonnay. There were two stalls in the lobby ladies' room and the line snaked out the door all

weekend long. "We should take over the men's room," attendees joked throughout, but we never did.

I had looked forward to the conference with an equal mix
of eagerness and dread. I've always had little tolerance for anything that involves large groups of women moving one another
to tears. I held out some hope of being transformed during
the weekend, of finding myself sitting next to an impossibly
inspiring woman and deciding, spur of the moment, to quit
my job and fly off to help people in some war-torn (but pictur-
esque) corner of the planet. Far likelier was that I would sit
through hours of heartrending interviews with rape victims in
the Congo and then return to my desk on Monday morning to
resume reporting a story about Fendi's $1,400 Lucite platform
stripper heels, which were proving to be *the* hot shoe for spring.

The Millennium Hotel is right in the middle of New York's
Theater District, around the corner from Town Hall and a
block east of Sardi's, the famous after-show meeting place
for Broadway stars. I put on my go-to black-tie dress in
the handicapped stall at work before heading uptown in a
Town Car with my colleagues. Our first official responsibility
was to act as hosts of the opening-night dinner, welcoming
guests, anchoring tables and chatting up delegates so everyone
felt comfortable and included. We had to fight through a
busy lobby full of disoriented tourists spooked by the rain. I
crammed into an elevator car with conference delegates on
their way to dinner and stray hotel guests returning in defeat
to their rooms. It smelled like damp novelty sweatshirts,
hot-dog breath and rosewater—a strange mix of boyish

pleasure-seeking scents and maternal problem-solving scents and sweat and mildew.

When we arrived on the eighth floor, the doors opened on an Epcot-like scene. In contrast to the high winds and hurricane-like conditions outside, the atmosphere in the room was subtropical: yellow lights, orange carpet, and everywhere you looked, the walls and pillars had been decorated with thick swarms of plastic monarch butterflies, swooping and twisting ninety feet above midtown. The tables were covered in orange and yellow cloths, with large bouquets of orange and yellow carnations in the center. The whole thing had an enchantingly girlish feel, like we were just occupying the room until Kimberly Whoever's sweet sixteen party started later that night. I half expected Melanne Verveer, the United States Ambassador-at-Large for Global Women's Issues and the evening's keynote speaker, to take the stage while a broad-based international orchestra played "Zip-a-Dee-Doo-Dah."

I was at table eleven, just behind the head table, where Tina, Diane and the guests of honor were to sit. I parked my things and waited, smoothing the wrinkles in my button-up silk dress and worrying that my lipstick had smudged. Three hundred fifty women draped in Chanel and St. John were in the process of loading into and unloading from the three small wood-paneled elevators. I tapped my fingers on the edge of a chair and watched as they chitchatted their way into the hall amid swarms of fake butterflies.

Over at the head table, a billionaire mogul caught my eye. He and I had met several times before, and I'd interviewed him once for the *Wall Street Journal*. He flashed a look of recognition and motioned for me to come over. He was chatting with a woman I didn't recognize, whom I assumed ran some sort of major global philanthropic organization. It was just a few paces to where he stood, and as I floated over, I reflected on how lucky I was to work for a great woman, to be at this monumental conference all about women's rights, to have the chance to meet all these illustrious Women in the World.

"Hi, [Mr. X]," I said.

Mr. X wore a suit that looked like it had been sewn onto his body. He had applied just the right amount of expensive cologne. He was dignified and calm, and as he leaned in close to my ear, I felt a measure of pride at having finally achieved a small level of recognition in the world. I did not think about Crown Heights in this moment because Crown Heights, and all its poverty and frumpiness and sporadic spousal abuse, did not exist in this moment. I smiled my best young professional lots-of-potential smile.

"I'll have a vodka tonic," he said.

I felt my ears turn hot and red. He pulled back and I looked in his eyes, the lots-of-potential smile frozen on my face.

He turned to the philanthropist woman and asked, "What do you want?"

"Ummmmm," she said, looking off in the direction of the butterflies. "I'll have vodka with a splash of soda."

I nodded, pained, and went off to find a waiter, who brusquely informed me there was no hard liquor on offer. So I did what any grown woman who'd aspired her entire life to be smart and sassy and formidable would have done. I went and hid in the bathroom until it was time for dinner.

When I was certain everyone had taken her seat and my mogul friend had forgotten about his drink, I crept out of the bathroom and into the light. It was a long walk to my table, past survivors of genocide and rape in Africa, founders of major philanthropic organizations, authors of great books. I gathered my strength as I moved from the bathroom toward table eleven. Maybe this was the solution, I thought. Maybe my life lived in deferment was deferring to the wrong thing. Maybe the universe does send me signs, and maybe the sign tonight pointed to a life of good deeds and charitable service, of rescuing rape victims and setting them up with microloans.

With each step I grew more hopeful that there was a path to righteousness and I was on it. Who knows: Whoever sat there at table eleven might hold the key to my future. She might look at me and see not a cocktail waitress, nor a fashion writer, but a wholly different person, bound for some life-affirming adventure. I was the present by the fireplace. Who could know what lay within!

I rounded the corner amid a swarm of plastic butterflies just as Melanne Verveer took the stage. Table eleven came into view, and I could see there was one seat open. All the women looked intently up at Ambassador Verveer, and I did too. I was fully swept up in the moment. Forget the vodka tonic, forget Carrie Bradshaw, forget Crown Heights. I was walking head-long into my future, and it was a future of great women. Women who helped women. A community of meaning.

I sat down in the seat and looked to my left.

Sitting there, smiling, was Candace Bushnell.

I stared at her for a full minute before collecting myself enough to speak. She looked beautiful. Her waist was the size of my pinkie. She wore a blue silk blouse that matched nicely with her eyes and a thin white fur vest over top—rabbit, I guessed. It was slim and soft. Dinner was a slab of lasagna that tasted like a beach towel soaked in marinara sauce. The creator of *Sex and the City* was occupying herself by graciously cutting the lasagna into small pieces and moving them around her plate so it appeared she had eaten some of it.

"Candace?" I said.

"Hi," she said. She was kind and friendly.

I said that it was wonderful—really, *so great*—to meet her. She smiled and nodded in a way that could have meant "Likewise" or "Somebody call security, please." In spite of myself, I started to fawn, expressing my admiration, thanking her for creating a modern female archetype that, however flawed, was superficial without being entirely substance-free. I said embarrassing things about how Carrie Bradshaw had been a totem to me, a kind of religious figure in my youth.

How many twenty-seven-year-olds must come up to Candace Bushnell every single day and talk to her like they were old friends, just because we can all recite full script pages of *Sex and the City* dialogue from memory?

Candace took all of this in. She was calm and polite.

My effusion ran on and drifted into the personal. I told her about my breakup. I told her about my rabbi. I told her about

Anya, the twenty-five-year-old mother of three who couldn't remember how old she was, and about how all the women in my neighborhood looked at me with such pity, like I was a washed-up old maid, and about how many wrong turns I'd taken on my way to this seat in this room with these people. I told her I was freaking out a little. I used the phrase "freaking out a little."

"How old are you?" she asked.

"Twenty-seven," I replied, catching my breath.

She thought for a moment.

"That's about right," she said.

All calm and cool.

All Zen Buddha–like.

(The woman to my right at dinner was a Zen Buddhist. "Richard Gere was telling me he switched to Tibetan Buddhism because Zen Buddhism didn't go deep enough," she told me later that night. A lot of her sentences began, "Richard Gere . . .")

Like a motherless maniac—like every other twenty-seven-year-old twit in shoes she can't afford—I had poured myself out into a puddle before Carrie Bradshaw herself. And filling the role she didn't choose but clearly has made peace with, as a lifestyle guru for all the lost girls who've modeled themselves in her fictionalized image, she did what she could. She didn't commend me. She didn't offer counsel. She didn't say whether this was a good thing or a bad thing, whether I should change or "lean in" or run away to Majorca or find a husband as soon as possible. "That's about right" was all she said.

"Okay," I said back, feeling mortified and also strangely comforted. I looked to Candace, but she had already turned her attention back to the stage. To my right, the Zen Buddhist sat ramrod straight, her focus on Melanne Verveer. I had no choice but to pass the rest of the evening this way, fidgeting between these two pools of serenity. Sometimes you get so close to your childhood vision of grown-up happiness that it scrambles the picture. You meet the messiah, and she's perfectly polite, but she's busy moving lasagna around her plate, listening to people with real problems.

"WOMEN IN THE WORLD" continued, in this fashion, for three days. I sat still, surrounded by Candace Bushnell and her cohort, patiently listening to the stories of women with a lot more to say than any of us had: There was Edna Anan Ismail, a native of Somaliland, who was eight years old when her family tied her down and "circumsized" her, cutting and stitching her vagina to the diameter of a matchstick. There was Marietou Diarra, a Senegalese woman whose eldest daughter died as a result of being circumcised. There was Kiran Bedi, India's first female police officer, talking of the country's sex trafficking victims, and Sunitha Krishnan, a former child sex slave turned antitrafficking activist, who was gang-raped by eight men at the age of sixteen. There was Annie Rashidi-Mulumba, who described the "sexual massacre" under way in the Congo. At some point, there was lunch. During lunch, *New York Times* columnist Thomas Friedman interviewed

Christine Lagarde, joking that his daughter should hook up with her son.

The last panel at "Women in the World" featured a handful of media types. The subject was "How do you make people pay more attention?" In a world full of people like me, who will pretty much listen to stories of female genital mutilation and sex trafficking only when they're trapped between a Zen Buddhist and Candace Bushnell, how do you get anyone to care about anything? How do you even get them to hear anything? "We probably can't look to Hollywood to save us," said Nora Ephron, my Hollywood hero, who arrived for the panel dressed in leather pants, looking ageless and perfect and exactly as I always imagined her to look. Next up was Lauren Zalaznik, the president of Bravo, the cable network that created the *Real Housewives* franchise of programs, in which rich women get drunk on Pinot Grigio and yank at each other's hair extensions, and also *Top Chef,* Cosmo's favorite reality show. Her advice, for those of us who were past the point of dedicating their lives to aiding the infirm but who maybe wanted to be slightly better human beings, was: "Do as much good in the world as you can, and make some money doing it."

I WENT TO WORK on Monday and wrote my story about Fendi's $1,400 Lucite platform stripper heels. I wish I could say the experience was soul crushing, but actually it was fun. I interviewed an erudite British stripper, who gave me lessons on walking in stilettos, and the creative director of *Elle* magazine, who gently suggested not everyone should wear these shoes. I wrote the piece and it went online, taking its place in my growing catalog of unapologetic fluff.

What was to apologize for, ultimately? It is such a luxury of a problem to expect to be made whole by your work. It is such an absurd indulgence to stay up at night, thinking that maybe if you had made different choices, you would be a better person, living a more profound and useful life. This is the life I wanted, and for better and worse it is the life I got. I paid my rent and supported myself in New York. I had a community of meaning, a beautiful one, full ditzy fashion people and brilliant eccentrics and lovely young mothers I met in Crown Heights. I tried to be a good person, to help people when I could and to not be too judgmental of people whose values were different from mine. Sometimes I succeeded at this and sometimes I failed.

Everything I knew felt half true. I hated Crown Heights, except the parts I loved. I adored Fashion Week, except that I also loathed it. I lived for my colleagues, worshipped Tina and Edward, was happy writing silly stories about Tiger Woods and stripper heels, but also felt a kind of hollowness in the abstract, that nagging pointlessness pulling at my clothes. If I could just get back to Manhattan, I caught myself thinking sometimes. If I could get away from the mice and return to civilization as I desired it to look, I would be okay. If I could just run away to Majorca. If I could just meet a new hero and start all over again. Again.

You think you have nothing tying you down except a job

and a few boxes of stuff in a shitty $650-a-month apartment and a rabbi who's a little too dramatic about his love life, but then you realize the whole thing is a lead balloon. You can spend your days saving lives or writing stories or studying Torah or practicing jujitsu and otherwise trying to resolve the mess, distill it into a clear focus. But it turns out the mess is the whole point. So you might as well dig down. Lean in. Make a home there.

Jujitsu Blonde

vs.

Big Oil

What are you doing this weekend? Edward said just before eleven one lovely spring morning in the Gehry boat.

"Working?"

"How would you feel about going to the Gulf?"

My flight left in four hours.

On April 20, an oil rig called *Deepwater Horizon* exploded in the Gulf of Mexico, about forty miles off the Louisiana coast, in the Macondo Prospect oil field. The explosion itself killed eleven workers on the rig, which was controlled by the British Petroleum company. It left a gaping hole at the bottom of the Gulf, from which oil was gushing into the water at a rate that was first estimated to be around 1,000 barrels per day and later revised up to 62,200 barrels in the first day of the spill. People started saying *Deepwater Horizon* was the biggest man-made natural disaster in American history, although it's always difficult to draw clear lines around such things. When do natural disasters start and when do they end, exactly? How many ripples out do you count—how many species of animals extinct or generations susceptible to exotic cancers? Are oil-suffocated birds and the destruction of hundreds of miles of freshwater wetlands better or worse than the nuclear devastation of Three Mile Island or Hiroshima, for that matter? In any event, it was bad. No one knew how to stop the spill, which had decimated the coast's fishing and tourist industries, and President Obama had imposed a moratorium on further drilling in the Gulf, paralyzing the region's last major business: oil.

My colleagues knew I lived with a rabbi in Brooklyn, but they joked that I really lived under my desk. The debate boiled down to semantics. If where you "live" is determined by where you pay rent, then I lived in Crown Heights, no question. But if it's determined by where you keep the majority of your wardrobe, they were absolutely right. My desk was in a corner, between two walls of windows overlooking the Hudson River and the West Side Highway. I had six vertical files and one small closet, and all were filled with clothes. Not once in all the time I lived in Brooklyn did I actually do laundry there. Instead, every week, I filled a tote bag with ten pounds of clothing and carried it to a wash-and-fold place three blocks from my office. When cornered by colleagues and asked what I was doing—as I, say, unloaded this week's wash into a filing cabinet—I would quietly confess to my private shame. In this respect above all others, New York had softened and sissified me. I could stand, rail straight, upside down for five minutes in yoga class, but I couldn't wash my own underwear.

Since the mouse incident, I had been spending more and more nights in the city, sleeping in Brooklyn less and less. What once had felt like an escape—like a dark, loud kosher cave I could crawl into to avoid my actual life—now felt like my actual life, and my escape increasingly was Manhattan. I lingered in the city after work, went to yoga, met up with friends and ended up crashing on their couches. Kate had a seafoam green futon in her living room, where I slept some-times with Bailey, her labradoodle, who would put his head on the pillow next to mine and snore. Rachel and her hus-band, Josh, a former Wall Street banker, had a plush sectional sofa and a limitless supply of Special K Red Berries in their two-story condo in Long Island City. Kristin, a designer, had a double-wide brown velvet couch in her Tribeca loft plus coconut macaroons from Whole Foods. Sara, a film execu-tive, had a stubborn dachshund named Muri, a one-bedroom with a patio on Sullivan Street in Soho and a boyfriend in Brooklyn with whom she stayed much of the time. Between these options and my office, I made a home. By summer, I was sleeping in Brooklyn only one or two nights a week. A friend called me La Vagabonda.

One night in Crown Heights, I was sitting in the living room, tapping away on my BlackBerry, when Cosmo marched out of his bedroom, carrying my copy of Michael Chabon's

The Amazing Adventures of Kavalier & Clay, opened to page 143. "Read this," he said, jabbing an index finger at a passage. I read aloud:

> "And you have to tell us how's come if you're from Japan, you could be Sammy's cousin and look like such a Jew," Davy O'Dowd said.
> "We're in Japan," Sammy said. "We're everywhere."
> "Jujitsu," Joe reminded him.
> "Good point," said Davy O'Dowd.

This was more literally true for Cosmo, who substituted a community of Jews with a community of jujitsu masters among whom he felt perfectly at home. For me, it was not Jews per se but people who felt, for one reason or another, like my people. They were scattered all over greater New York, and they fed me and put me up for the night as I wandered around that spring and summer, half homeless, afraid of being eaten by mice. You collect these people, like reverse osmosis, as you go through life. Drawing toward you people who are not your blood but are your family. At Sara's apartment, I kept a toiletry bag and two dresses. At Kate's, a full complement of yoga gear. And under my desk at work, which was my primary home away from home, I kept nine pairs of shoes.

This made it easy to pack for a weeklong trip to Louisiana set to begin four hours hence. A few colleagues gathered to point and laugh as I crawled around my desk area, selecting summer dresses and pumps for my trip south. By midafternoon, I was in a Town Car to JFK, with a jam-packed travel bag in the trunk. (I kept a travel bag near the printer.) By midnight, I was on Bourbon Street.

Here was my chance to do something good.

NEW ORLEANS IS the only other place in America I'd ever seriously considered living, and it has always lingered in my memory as an object of fading desire, a road not taken. After my sophomore year in college, I worked on the metro desk of the New Orleans *Times-Picayune*, an intensely quirky regional newspaper that would go on to win a Pulitzer Prize for its coverage of Hurricane Katrina. My first assignment during my intern summer was in the East Jefferson bureau, where I covered such headline-making news as the last day of elementary school and the annual return of a flock of purple martins—a not especially handsome species of migratory bird—to a local bridge. On my first day of work, a photographer took me on a tour of Metairie, the neighborhood in "East Jeff" where our bureau was located. Metairie was a largely white, middle-class area composed of drive-through daiquiri shacks, po'boy shops, closed-up movie theaters and churches in strip malls. "Are you a member of the tribe?" the photographer asked at one point during our tour. "Do you mean, am I a Jew?" I asked, frightened. He said yes, and I said yes, and in response to that, he took a sharp right and drove me through a crowded neighborhood of split-level homes, ultimately pulling up to one that looked no different from any of the others. "This is where David Duke lives," he said.

My boss in the bureau had lost half his index finger in a lawn mower accident and spent most of the day gnawing on the nub. One of my three fellow reporters was a blond, motherly type who gave me unsolicited dieting tips like "Eat absolutely nothing sweet after three p.m." I cried every day for my first two weeks because all my friends were in New York or Washington that summer, and I was stuck in some sweat-drenched nightmare, covering high school baseball games with no friends except a photographer suspiciously knowledgeable about anti-Semites.

It took time for me to realize that the beauty of New Orleans is in its languor, and because I was training to be a New Yorker, I fought it for a while. I fought against the humidity, complaining that coming to the city was like crawling into the mouth of a Saint Bernard. I fought against the pace of life, the slow lurch of traffic, the imprecision, the way it took forever to get anything done. I wanted specifics. I wanted the old lady in the faded pink shotgun house to shut up about her grandchild already and answer my questions about the fire down the street, because that way—the logic went—I could finish my work for the day and somehow get back North sooner, and somehow graduate sooner and go to New York. One by one, I fought against the daily rhythms of a place that seemed to slur its way through time, and what took some time to realize was that the slur is the whole point.

I lived with an M.D./Ph.D. student named Ralston and his girlfriend, a circus acrobat, in a dilapidated house on Fern Street, a few blocks away from Tulane University and its rows of fraternity houses. At night you could see cockroaches crawling around in the cracks of our front stoop, which gave me the idea—correct, I'm sure—that the entire framework of the house was teeming with roaches, that if you were to peel back one of the walls, millions would spill out. There was also a particularly insidious subspecies of cockroach, which someone had given the deceptively sweet name palmetto bug. Palmettos had wings and would fly directly at your face. At first I fought them and cried when I lost, and then I gave in to them, like everything else. I submitted to the heat, to the slow turning of pointless fans, to long afternoons going nowhere, doing little. I knew almost no one in the city, so I had infinite stretches of solitude.

Of course, the city itself, and the broader American South, has a mythology of its own and a filmic quality that easily rivals New York or LA. But I had never read those books or watched those movies as a kid. They were beside the point. I went to New Orleans that summer because it was the job I had gotten, and my other choice was to go back to Pittsburgh and resume my post at the Andy Warhol Museum, where I had worked as a "gallery attendant" in high school, earning $6.53 an hour to ask children not to touch the paintings and Japanese tourists to please refrain from taking flash photographs—responsibilities I almost always performed stoned. The *Times-Picayune* gig, which paid $600 a week, was a relative windfall.

It wasn't until later that I read *A Confederacy of Dunces* and *Jitterbug Perfume* and watched *Midnight in the Garden of Good and Evil*, not until much later that I sobbed through the ending of *The Heart Is a Lonely Hunter*, which is not a book about New Orleans but about isolation and longing in hot dusty places, and made a pilgrimage five blocks from Chad's apartment in Brooklyn Heights to the house where Carson McCullers had lived. I arrived in the South in the summer of 2002 uninitiated and annoyed at this detour from the Eastern Seaboard; I left under duress, not wanting to go.

New Orleans, for me, begins at ten o'clock on a Tuesday night at the Maple Leaf Bar on Oak Street, with a bottle of Abita and a game of incompetent pool already behind me, another to come. Anyone who knows anything about the city knows, at a minimum, that the name of the place is "New ORlins" or "Nawlins" or any variation that is not "New OrLEENS" and that Rebirth plays Tuesday nights at the Maple Leaf. Rebirth is Rebirth Brass Band, which was less a band than a parade. It felt and certainly sounded like there were more people up on the Maple Leaf's small stage in its cramped main room under its original, ornate, pressed-metal ceiling than there were out in the audience. You got to the Maple Leaf early enough to get a spot in the first couple of rows, which guaranteed you would be hearing through cotton for the next few days, after the first six minutes of "Feel Like Funkin' It Up," whose only lyric, repeated over and over between horn solos, was:

Feel like funkin' it up!
Aahhhhhh, feel like funkin' it up!
Ahhhhh . . .

And then after, or before, there are fried oysters and fried catfish and maybe also some fried chicken at Jacques-Imo's, the unironically kitschy restaurant down the street, with the red-and-white-polyester tablecloths and the waiters who will offer you a free dessert just for the pleasure of watching you keep eating. And then, depending on how long these activities take, either before or after all that—depending on whether evening stretches into morning or the night bends to the will of the afternoon—you go to the Columns Hotel on St. Charles to drink Bloody Marys with the old New Orleans blue bloods and watch the trolley car pass and smell their cigar smoke and just *sit* for a spell. Time in New Orleans gives this way, forward and backward, pliant to everyone's whims. Everything gets done—the drinking here and eating there and more drinking and music and food and booze—with the day slowing up at some point and life just sinking down, settling in.

My second assignment was in Orleans Parish, at the newspaper's headquarters near the city's Central Business District. I covered the night cops beat Tuesday through Saturday, coming in around lunchtime and listening to a police scanner for news. Usually very little happened, and the highlight of my shift was the nightly lecture from the hair-netted cafeteria lady when I ordered my regular turkey on wheat about why didn't I have the gumbo or whatever they were serving under a congealed layer of grease. "Turkey gives you gas," she said.

But every once in a while I'd get lucky, and something horrible would happen. This was my chance to shine. This was when I first learned the essentially parasitic nature of journalism: that we thrive on other people's misery. The last day of elementary school in Metairie—all those adorable, inarticulate seven-year-olds who can't speak a quotable sentence to save their lives—were hell compared to the amphetamine boost of a murder-suicide. It was during my time in Orleans Parish—somewhere between the time in July when a man accidentally burned down a nice white house with three young children inside it and the time in August when a school group fell into a shark tank at the aquarium—that I fell in love. You never get inured to the tragedy, nor should you, but there is a special privilege in the telling of it. We have to bear witness to history, even ugly and tragic history like the pointless death of three little girls, and so writing these stories felt important to me, sad as they were.

The city is full of terrible poverty, racism, crime and injustice, which I saw when I was not submitting to the pulls of the French Quarter, when I was earning my $600 a week on the metro desk. Sometimes I went on "ride-alongs" with police officers, sitting behind the wire mesh in their cop cars, where the criminals usually sat, and going with them on their rounds. One night, I was reporting a story about the city's curfew law, which required all minors to be indoors after ten p.m. As far as I could tell, the city used this law to round up poor black children and force their parents, many of whom were single mothers working multiple jobs, to retrieve them. On my ride-along, we strayed from one of New Orleans's seven major housing projects only when we were en route to another. We never, for example, drove through my neighborhood, where white kids sometimes stayed out playing in the street until dawn.

On very rare occasions, my hazy life that summer came into sharp focus, as on the morning I met the mother of two of the three children who died in a fire in her white shotgun house. The fire was sparked by a faulty air conditioner left running while she and her boyfriend ducked out for a bit. All three children were under three years old. One left a pink tricycle toppled over in the front yard, and it was such a stark, obvious symbol of loss that when I saw it, the first thing I thought was, "Nah, not believable." The mother, herself only twenty, spoke to me through tears when I found her at a friend's house around the block. The house had been decorated for one of the girls' birthdays. It was now "veiled for a funeral," I wrote for the next day's front page, taking note of the tricycle and other details that earned praise from my editors over beers in the Quarter that night. This is the New Orleans the rest of America saw in the wake of Hurricane Katrina: the fortunate ones on higher ground and the unfortunate ones in the low-lying slums, decadence and depravity side by side.

If you go into journalism with some vague idea of helping people or in some way serving the greater good—and no

matter how preoccupied you may be with fashion and entertainment or blood and guts; the prettier, cleaner things in life
or the darker, dirtier ones, you always to some extent want to
do good—then New Orleans is a better destination than
most. There is a lot of good that needs doing there, and unlike
in New York, where you can go an entire lifetime leaping from
one luxury high-rise to another, in New Orleans the need is
manifest. Every place in America has its beauty and its tragedy, its heartbreaking stories to tell. In New Orleans, the stories are just easier to see.

I've had a good half-dozen journalism jobs since then, and
all have taught me something about the craft and something
about life: At the *Washington Post*—which gave America Deep
Throat, Watergate and the end of the Nixon administration—
I learned how to write a proper lede and also how to give a
proper blow job, the latter from a secret seventeen-page document written by a gay senior reporter and posted under an
innocuous title on the newspaper's internal server. At the *New
York Observer*, I learned that all journalism is really about
hubris and that "New York is Paris, kid" and that if you walk
into enough parties pretending like you belong, someday
maybe you will. From the *New York Times*, where I accepted a
job that I quit before starting, I learned that great newspapers
are made by many smart, kind, hardworking people and,
invariably, a few chimpanzees. At the *Wall Street Journal*, I
learned humility and what EBIDTA stands for. At the *Daily
Beast* I learned a little about genius and a lot about madness

and that as far as free chocolate pudding is concerned, I prefer Swiss Miss to Jell-O.

My brief stint at the *Times-Picayune* taught me some of the least useful things I know: what brain matter looks like on the cement floor of someone's government-subsidized living room; how to recognize the smell of burned baby hair; what to do if you're cut and bleeding in a small tank teeming with sharks; the best place to hear zydeco on a Monday night that'll also give you a paper plate of red beans, sausage and rice at the door; where to go for boudin and crawfish étouffée; how to sit for five hours in a hot coffee shop and enjoy it; how to spot nutria rats in the swampland on the Mississippi border; how to dance to jazz. I learned these things and learned also that they were worth knowing, and then, before the implications of that second lesson began to take hold, I left. I made my way to New York, and that was the end of that.

WHEN I CAME BACK, five years later, on assignment from the *Beast*, the city at first appeared unchanged. Louis Armstrong International Airport was still barren, still over-air-conditioned and still smelled violently of mildew. Bourbon Street was still brimming with the worst of humanity, drunk and obese, one of whom grabbed my ass and said, "Where's the party?" when I went out for a walk the night I arrived. I was booked at the Hotel Monteleone, two blocks off Bourbon, in the heart of the Quarter. I was staying, oddly, in a two-room

suite on the eleventh floor, with a bedroom, sitting room, and
two bathrooms, one of which had a Jacuzzi tub. The room
cost ninety-nine dollars a night and came with two Andes
mints and a handwritten note from the maid each afternoon.
My task while in town was twofold: to tell a more human side
of the oil-spill story, where other media outlets had tended to
dwell on the technical and the easily defined—gallons lost,
species annihilated, flaws in different proposed solutions—
and also, if possible, to catch someone important "in the act."

BP being a British company, the spill provided an opportunity to dust off treasured story lines about Old England and
its uneasy relationship with the West. BP's uppermost managers were British, its upper-uppermost being the pale, thin-
lipped and uniquely unsympathetic Tony Hayward, who days
after an explosion that took eleven lives and untold thousands
of livelihoods, complained to an interviewer about the burdens
of his company's crisis-management strategy, saying, "I just
want to get back to my life." The day I arrived in New Orleans,
Tony Hayward left, flying straight back to England after
enduring hours of withering congressional hearings and entire
days sweltering in Louisiana. He left for a "much-needed rest,"
and where he went was the Isle of Wight, where he watched his
yacht, *Bob*, compete in a race sponsored by J.P.Morgan Asset
Management. It would not have been any worse if the yacht
were named *Blue Collar Bill* or *Ha Ha, I Named My Boat After
Some Generic Dirty Prole*. Wouldn't it have been great to catch
him at a strip club, say, or tearing through a steak at Gala-
toire's? This was the assignment. New Orleans is Sin Central,

and the British are colonists at heart, and wouldn't it be interesting journalistically if Tony Hayward or any of his tweedy
deputies, all no doubt eager to get back to their lives, were
quietly sampling any of the local culture?

The next level of BP managers under Hayward were swarthy Texans, led by Robert "Bob" Dudley, the chief operating
officer and, who knows, perhaps the namesake for the yacht.
Dudley and his charges were drawling, jeans-wearing, brush-
clearing, get-down-to-business types in the mold of George
W. Bush, and the emerging media narrative held that these
were the people who understood the situation, who were kins-
men to the people affected and therefore should be in charge.
President Obama, flaccid and as seemingly peeved by the oil-
spill distraction as Tony Hayward, eventually mustered a show
of pique, asking his staff to find him an "ass to kick." But by
then a special American brand of nostalgia had already set in,
and we were already back to wanting cowboys in charge. Hayward was eventually reassigned, first removed from a position
of oversight of the *Deepwater Horizon* disaster and then relo-
cated to Siberia—overseeing BP's emerging business with
Russia. The president's due would come in the midterm elec-
tions, people said. This was "Obama's Katrina."

My flight from New York was nearly empty. My closest
neighbor was an engineer who spent the entire trip working on
a complex-looking blueprint. When we arrived, I asked if he
was working on a project to cap the oil spill, and he shook his
head sadly. "I design coffee filters." We walked together out to
the taxi stand, where two hundred cabs were lined up in neat

rows, waiting for passengers. My driver, Mohammed, said he had been waiting four hours for my thirty-dollar fare to downtown New Orleans. He was Pakistani and had moved twenty years ago to Hawaii, then to Louisiana because, although the weather was beautiful in Honolulu, it was a tough place to make a living. He lived in New Orleans with his brother, his wife and his two daughters and their families. I told him I was from New York and he perked up. "I hear you can earn money there year-round," he said. Tourist season, such as it had been, was long over in New Orleans. I asked how the oil spill compared to Hurricane Katrina, and Mohammed said, "Much worse."

He gave me a version of the same explanation I heard from many people while I was there—the beignet chef on her cigarette break outside Café du Monde; the people behind the counter at a butcher shop in the Faubourg Marigny; my friend Eric, a New Orleans blue blood, whom I met for brunch one morning—which is that with Katrina you could see the devastation. After the floodwaters receded, at least you could drive around or flip on the TV or, God forbid, go buy a newspaper and actually look at what had happened, connect with the suffering and understand, physically, what needed to be done. Entire neighborhoods needed to be rebuilt; the entire infrastructure of the city needed to be knocked on, tested and probably stripped to the bone—but it was visible and because it was visible, with enough grit and enough of an outpouring of support from the rest of the country, it was also doable. What was the *Deepwater Horizon* explosion? It was some dark sludge glugging out into the Gulf of Mexico forty miles south. There weren't any puppies stranded on roofs. Anderson Cooper and Shepard Smith weren't weeping on the Interstate. The oil spill was slowly decimating the topography of the state's southern coast. It was wiping out the seafood industry that made up so much of the local diet and culture. It was gathering on the outskirts of town, ready to be lifted by high winds and dropped like a big wet stinking veil on New Orleans proper as soon as hurricane season came. But other than one slide show of gunky birds that made the rounds shortly after the spill, you couldn't *see* anything.

I rented a silver Kia and drove around. In Houma, where many of the cleanup workers were stationed, I met Big Al of Big Al's Seafood Restaurant (as distinguished from Big Al of Big Al's Malibu Beach Bar), who offered me a drink, told me about how his business was suffering and repeatedly apologized for the skin cancer removal scars on his nose. In Grand Isle, a blue-collar vacation community on the southeastern tip of the state and what was being called the Ground Zero of the spill, I met Ruth of Ruth's Diner, a small, sweet woman with sad eyes who had lived in the same place for the last fifty-five years. She had met her husband in Grand Isle, and they had been married fifty-four years ago, and he had died last year. Her diner was empty and would probably stay that way. Her health was fading and her children were encouraging her to move. "Where am I gonna go?" she asked. "My husband is buried here, and I'm not leaving him." I drove all along the coast, stuck my toes in the water, talked to cleanup workers and aid workers and fisherman and oilmen and mothers and daughters whose lives were upended by the spill. But in a week's time, I didn't *see* anything that looked like the end of the world, even though for thousands of people, it surely was.

While I was waiting for my silver Kia to be ready for pickup at the Budget Rental Center down the street, I popped into a consignment store in the Quarter and tried on a few hats and one sequined floral jacket, like Rue McClanahan would have worn on the *Golden Girls*. The shop smelled like the attic of the grandmother I never had, and it was all on sale for pretty much whatever you wanted it to be. I went to pay for the jacket and that's where I met Justin, who ran the shop with his boyfriend. We got to talking, and it turned out Justin was a fashion hound. I came back that night to return an umbrella he'd lent me, and we got to talking again.

We drank a bottle of rosé and smoked cigarettes on the back patio of his shop and discussed the last three seasons of Marc Jacobs's collections, and the expansion of the Band of Outsiders label, and the potential python shortage in Florida. It was a Tuesday night, I flew out the next morning. I had been working so much, all I'd had was fast food and room service that week, and I convinced him to accompany me for one proper night on the town. We went for fried chicken at Jacques-Imo's, and then passed by the Maple Leaf, where Rebirth was going onstage. Time sank down like a feather bed. I could have gone in to listen. I could have missed my flight the next day. It was all there, laid out before me, and it was so far from mouse-infested Brooklyn. I could have crashed there for a while, or stayed, even—found work, dug in and succumbed again. Instead I drove Justin home, arguing about Alexander Wang the entire time, and the next morning, I arrived at the airport with an hour to spare.

I wrote my stories and I came home to discover that some of them had been well received, and maybe even helped humanize the suffering on the Gulf Coast, judging by a few supportive comments left on the *Beast*'s website. And then there was the one I did about BP employees flirting with waitresses at the Houma Hooters—and all the other awkward enjambments that occur when British geologists commingle with sweet-faced Southerners—which had so incensed the people of Houma that someone created a Facebook group just to tear apart the story. A local newspaper columnist wrote an entire piece about how I had misunderstood the situation, overemphasizing the friendly attitudes some residents felt toward BP and underreporting the enmity between the two sides. It was about the same ratio of positive comments to vitriol that I was used to, and I felt the usual mix of pride and shame at the pieces of writing I had churned out, magnified slightly in both directions. It had been good to run away to New Orleans for a week, and I was happy I'd done it, and I wanted to do it again someday. But was I transformed? No.

"Running away is never the answer," Madeleine says. "Because wherever you go, it'll still be *you* there."

And being me, I still found the person who could talk about the python shortage.

We're in Japan. We're everywhere.

I could run away to Crown Heights or Los Angeles or New Orleans or anywhere, and maybe I could even do something more meaningful when I got there, but wherever I went, I was really just me: a two-time Space Camp graduate with an unnatural interest in dyeing her hair and an unhealthy preoccupation with expensive shoes. I am no more an altruist than I am a perfect collage of all the women I admired as a kid. I'm just a person who sometimes, in between all the bouts of narcissism and loneliness, tries to do something good, and who usually ends up finding someone to talk to about the hottest designers or what Marc Jacobs is showing for spring. It's not the woman I always dreamed I'd be, but actually, it's not too far off.

Things of Wisdom

There are many things I learned during my time in Crown Heights, but none of them was how to live with mice. We all have our limitations. I always thought it would be the people who drove me out, but in the end, it was the people I stayed for, as long as I possibly could. Then summer came. And I had no air conditioner. And the idea of sitting around sweltering in this mouse-infested room was more than I could bear. Strangely, Cosmo never saw a mouse in his room. They haunted only me.

I was ready to move back to Manhattan. I had made peace with my life. I worried about Cosmo. What would happen to him now that he was a bacon-scarfing jujitsu blue belt and one step closer to becoming an American? Would his story carry him to the place where my story began, where the limitless possibilities of life in Manhattan in the twenty-first century collapsed like a tower on his head? I hoped not. I wanted to protect him, but who can really protect anyone? We would stay friends at least, I hoped.

One afternoon at work, I went online and searched for a studio somewhere downtown. Ashes to ashes, Craigslist to Craigslist. The first listing that appeared was for a tiny one-bedroom walk-up in Nolita, a small neighborhood encompassing the area just north of what used to be Little Italy. I wrote to the e-mail address in the ad, and the response came back immediately.

"When can you come see the apartment?" it said. It was signed "Moses."

"Is your name really Moses?" I wrote back.

"Yes. —Moses."

I reminded myself of certain immutable truths: The universe does not send us signs. We are not in dialogue with the universe. Jews run the real estate business in Manhattan, and if he weren't Moses, he would have been Abraham or Isaac or Jacob—or Cosmo. If he had been Cosmo, it really would have shaken my lack of faith.

We set up a time for me to see the apartment, and on the appointed day, it poured. I canceled, and when I tried to reschedule, Moses never wrote me back.

On the third day of my apartment search, after several other missed connections in downtown Manhattan rental real estate, I looked in the *New York Times*. There was a studio on East 11th Street, reasonably priced, with a renovated kitchen and bath. I wrote to the real estate agent. He replied. Robert. *Phew.*

I made an appointment to meet Robert during the two-hour window he was showing the apartment and arrived five minutes late. Robert was already on his way back to the office, but I called and begged him to come back. "Whatever it looks like, I'll take it," I said. It was roughly a thousand degrees outside, and I was tired of schlepping around in the heat. He led me upstairs to the tiny fifth-floor studio, with a pink bathtub, a built-in air conditioner and eggshell-colored walls. It was small and innocuous and not in any way metaphorical or evocative of biblical times, not in any way like my old West Village apartment, beset by plagues and ultimately drowned in a flood. This was just a plain old studio—my own little place, three subway stops or one short mile from where I started but an infinite distance in space and time from the life I once had lived.

"I'll take it," I said.

"You haven't even seen the best part," Robert replied. He beckoned me over to one of the studio's two windows, which looked out over a fire escape. On the fire escape was a nest, and in the nest was a dove.

COSMO TOOK THE NEWS of my leaving in stride. Then again, it's hard to care about much of anything when you're head over heels in love.

They'd met at a barbecue in early June. She was tall, slim,

with red hair; a shiksa. "She drinks, smokes, smokes pot," he'd said the next day, while cartoon bluebirds fluttered above his head. They had gotten drunk in his friend's backyard, swearing and speaking Russian all night. She had come as the date of another friend. She was some other guy's girl. But she had huddled with Cosmo next to the grill and traded dirty jokes with him and gotten up occasionally to fetch him a beer. They had—yes, kissed.

It was all happening so fast. He was drafting Tolstoyan e-mails, spending hours crafting Facebook messages he almost never actually sent, worrying about what they would do on their dates. She was waiting days before responding, dashing off clipped, ambiguous replies, promising to meet him places, then bailing at the last minute. For their second date, she invited him to dinner, and when he arrived, her entire extended family was there.

"I'm not even sure it was a date," he said breathlessly. "She barely spoke to me the whole night."

Love, it was love, *love*! Heartbreaking love, impossible love, terrific agonizing Russian love, the kind that makes you forget about food, about work, about anything but smoking and drinking and *her* for days. Vera was everything Cosmo had ever wanted in a woman: irreligious, boozy, aloof. This was not a nice Jewish girl who'd marry him and have his kids, this was the sort of woman who tempted you and teased you and drove you crazy for years on end until you couldn't take it anymore—the uncertainty, the deception, the jealous rage— and, in the throes of final desperation, just to make the pain stop, one night maybe you drank enough vodka to blind an army, then staggered through the streets crying her name, then screwed up the courage to throw yourself under an oncoming subway train. For the first full week of his infatuation, Cosmo didn't once mention Vera's boobs—it didn't matter.

What should he do? he asked over and over. Should he write or not write? Call or not call? Tell her exactly how he feels, lay it on the line, profess his love?

"You should date other women," I said.

"I will never date another woman," he said. He nodded his head vigorously up and down, a giddy smile slapped across his face.

Cosmo turned thirty-one on a rainy, miserable day in July. He threw himself a small party at a beer garden near Crown Heights. Vera was nowhere to be found.

"What does she do for a living?" I asked.

"She buys death," he said.

"She what, huh?"

"She buys the remainders of people's life insurance policies, once they get tired of paying for them. They have a doctor who evaluates the people and determines how much longer they're going to live, and if it's not that long, they buy the person out of his policy and then collect once he kicks the bucket."

"Wow," I said. "Sexy."

"*I know.*"

Cosmo's dream girl was the Grim Reaper. She occupied all his thoughts. He spent long hours hovered on the edge of the giant oak dining room table, feet propped on the windowsill, dragging off hand-rolled cigarettes, lighting his next one with his last. He was quoting *War and Peace*. There was no end to joyous misery.

"I am falling apart at the seams," he said, and the way he said it, it sounded like bragging.

"Do you know, I've been walking right on the edge of the subway platform, right by where the train comes," he said. "Even when it's very busy and would be easy for me to fall in. It used to be I was afraid to do things like that, but not now for some reason."

The night I told him I was moving out was intolerably hot, well into the nineties. A family of rats the size of Pomeranians was running around in the cement courtyard below our kitchen window, but otherwise, all living creatures had retreated inside, underground, out of town—anywhere cooler. Instead of air-conditioning, our fourth-floor apartment had two small plastic window fans that pushed around damp, sweat-laden currents of air. This produced the opposite of a chill. The fans made the apartment seem even more swamplike and fetid by providing fresh reminders of heat, sending warm, slow gusts against the skin. The effect was like slapping a bruise. Cosmo, cooking dinner over two gas burners set to high, barely acknowledged my entrance. A half-smoked cigarette, trailing a full inch of ash, hung from a dead hand at his side.

"Hey, Cosmo, I think I found a new place in the city."

"Oh yeah?" he said morosely. "Great."

"What's up?" I said, wilting onto a kitchen chair.

What was up? Nothing. It was all down, down. Vera hadn't acknowledged his existence in more than a week. It was hot. He was miserable.

Every time I saw Cosmo for the next week, he was even worse: gloomier, more depressed, increasingly resigned to his lot. The temperature hovered around 100 degrees, the humidity near 100 percent. A sticky glaze formed on your skin on the walk to the subway in the morning and stayed there all day, morphing into a kind of ashy coating once you spent enough time in air-conditioning. It was impossible to feel clean, impossible to breathe through your nose without gagging. I dreamed of swimming pools and woke to the sound, as always, of the couple next door screaming at each other in Yiddish.

Then, on the worst, hottest, most unlivable afternoon of the whole summer, while I was at work, an e-mail came:

HA!

HA!

guess what? I just got an e-mail from vera. guess how it
starts? "my dear friend . . ." and then "where were you
saturday night, what are you up to, and bla-bla-bla"
it might be too early to tell, but preliminary reports
indicate that i might be singing and dancing.

We met up for dinner in the East Village the day after I moved out. I picked the restaurant, an organic, fair-trade, locavore café half a block from my new apartment, the sort of place that serves five-dollar mini-plates of braised Brussels sprouts handpicked by legal immigrants at a family farm upstate. We arranged to meet at eight. I arrived early and sat outside. He arrived early and sat at the bar. It took us twenty minutes to find each other, and by the time we did, I was on the verge of collapse. A stomach bug had descended that afternoon. As with our first dinner, I had no energy and no appetite.

I was sitting on a refurbished white shabby-chic wood bench, sinking ever closer to the pavement, when Cosmo appeared above me.

"Hi," he said. "This place is no good."

My body was now in open revolt, and I would have canceled earlier in the day, but Cosmo was skipping jujitsu for this, and by the time the nondescript ooky feeling in my gut graduated to a full-blown GI assault, it was too late to back out.

Hipsters swarmed around us—boys in corduroy cutoffs with ironic calf tattoos; girls in sundresses with wide stripes of fake blond sun streaks in their hair—ticking down their forty-five-minute waits, tracing circles in each other's palms. The August heat was breaking, and we were just on the verge of perfect weather in New York. It was still a few degrees too hot, though, still cloying and muggy. A light fog of city stench rose upward from a nearby sewer grate, mingling with the smell of freshly grilled sweet corn on the cob and fried country potatoes steaming out of the kitchen vent, down onto the sidewalk.

Cosmo clarified his request: "Is there anywhere around here that makes a good burger?"

We walked off toward First Avenue, where, one by one, Cosmo deemed a strip of restaurants either too crowded or too fancy or not in possession of the right kinds of beer. He stopped and pointed enthusiastically at a halal food truck on the corner opposite the Islamic Council of America. "Absolutely not," I said, gripping my stomach. In the neon glow of a skate shop, he took note of the greenish pallor of my skin.

"We have an expression in Russian," he said. "You've been hugging the white friend."

On the edge of Tompkins Square Park was a nearly empty French restaurant called Flea Market Café, with a twelve-dollar burger on the menu and a passable array of beers. One enormous gay man with a thick neck ringed in tribal tattoos was trading blow-job stories, sotto voce, with a gal pal by the window. To their right were two petite French women, running forks idly through a crème brûlée. It was one of their birthdays, and the blown-out candle still stood in the middle of the dessert. I pointed to the table to the left of the BJ duet.

"We're eating here."

Cosmo nodded and squeezed in next to the muscle-bound hunk, while I slumped down beside his friend and asked the waiter for a ginger ale. Cosmo handed me a pay stub and a letter from Social Security, both of which had arrived in the mail for me that morning. Then he pulled Thomas Mann's *Doctor Faustus* out of his bag and offered it reluctantly. It was the last book he'd borrowed. He found the writing "dry and difficult," which is the morose Russian rabbi equivalent of a teenage girl finding something "cute." He had spent the previous two weekends camped out, reading it, in Central Park but wasn't done yet.

Doctor Faustus, like any Faust story, is about a man who sells his soul to the devil in exchange for some earthly gift. In Mann's version, the protagonist, a composer, gives it up for music. His immortal life buys him temporary access to divine inspiration, allowing him to write melodies wholly unlike any written before. I read the book in college, in tandem with Martin Heidegger's *Being and Time*, and spent many hours, with and without the assistance of marijuana, barely understanding a word. The paper that resulted was a triumph of footnoting, with most of its insights dug out of long-neglected secondary works gathering dust in the Yale library. I read *Doctor Faustus* again after graduation, and without the pressure of "bringing *language* as *language* to *language*," in Heidegger's words, I actually liked it. It's a cautionary tale against extremism, against junking all established forms and starting over from scratch. On one level, it's a nice book about why we should all be afraid of Nazis. On another level, it's an argument against disengagement, against all those who stood around and allowed this idiot to sell his soul, setting off a chain reaction that (spoiler alert!) hurt everyone in the end. It's an indictment of those who go unquestioningly through life. It's an argument in favor of fucking with God.

After *War and Peace*, Cosmo had asked for another book, and I gave him the choice between that and *Valley of the Dolls*.

We studied the menu a minute in silence while our neighbors discussed ball-cupping technique. The waiter came to take our order. I had the wheat toast with avocado chunks, lemon juice and hot pepper flakes, minus the hot pepper flakes, plus water with no ice. Cosmo had a burger and a beer.

"How do you want the burger cooked?" the waiter asked, staring out the front door and fingering the full fringe of silver loops that lined the outside of his right ear.

Cosmo stared at me with big, unsure eyes.

"Medium," I said.

"What kind of beer?"

Cosmo scanned the menu and found nothing he liked, so he ordered the one he didn't recognize: a pale German wheat beer, the kind bars serve with a ladylike sliver of lemon on the lip of the glass. I suggested maybe something darker, and he nodded in agreement. This was dinner. It arrived suspiciously quickly, as if someone had preordered. Before taking a bite, Cosmo picked up the salt and set to work. He shook out a layer thick enough to maintain its whiteness even after being absorbed into the burger grease on both sides of the half-pound patty, plus a solid dousing of salad and fries.

"Oh God, you motherless boy," I said. "Promise me you'll eat the greens."

"I promise."

"I worry."

"Remember when you yelled at me about the bacon?" He took the biggest possible bite of the burger, stretching his jaws to their absolute limit, then chewed. "I will never make that mistake again."

"Remember we cooked pasta my first night?"

"If I never eat pasta again, it will be too soon," he said.

"I taught you about al dente."

"And it has been that way ever since." Seven minutes. He sets a timer.

He told me about Vera, who was having Lasik surgery this week. He told me he had decided to suspend training for his motorcycle license. In four to eight months, his papers would come through and maybe he'd pick it up again then.

"My old friend the heroin addict across the hall has been kicked out," he said.

"For not paying his rent?"

"Yes, if you can imagine. He came to the copy shop today, and my boss bought him lunch, and I saw him after, and I said, 'Chaim, why heroin? Why not alcohol? They're both depressants. Why not get drunk on twenty or thirty dollars a day instead of getting high on sixty or seventy?' And he said, 'Alcohol destroys your liver, man.'"

The check arrived, I paid, we left. Invigorated by the avocado and toast, I led Cosmo to a dessert place around the block. He shuffled down the street in agony.

"Dude," I said, "this is very exciting. You're in love."

"Is it!"

"Look: You're even more miserable than usual. You've been dragging yourself around like death for weeks. I think she might be the one."

"Fuck," he said, then paused for a minute to think. "Motherfucker! You may be right."

It was nine-thirty. We walked in silence through the hazy

evening, no one noticing as we passed. In Manhattan, under the streetlamp glare, under the starless sky, Cosmo and I were invisible. He wore a bluish-gray Uniqlo T-shirt and jeans, dark glasses, his hair cut short, and his beard shorn down to a punk-rock nub. I wore jeans, a shirt.

"I think I'm giving up on Hollywood," he said.

"Why?"

"I just saw this movie with John Travolta, *From Paris with Love*. It was terrible." The movie was about an American spy who teams up with a young Parisian to prevent a terrorist attack. Its tagline was "Two agents. One city. No merci." Cosmo had downloaded it on the Internet and watched it one night in his bedroom.

"I'm not sure you should give up on all American movies just because of one bad John Travolta action flick."

"Even still."

"What will you watch, then?"

"Foreign films."

"This from the guy who can recite every word of *Top Chef* season six."

Cosmo and I continued to meet every few months for cheeseburgers and dessert. A few weeks after I moved out, he found a new roommate to replace me, a Mexican lesbian, and eventually had to evict her because she stopped paying her rent and brought two other Mexican lesbians in to live on the couch. He kept plugging along at Fast Trak while the final paperwork for his green card went through. He was still doing jujitsu. He was still trying to get me to do jujitsu.

"I think my phase of falling apart is coming to a close," he said that summer night in the East Village, while we waited in line at the vegan bakery for some nondairy ice cream and a green tea macaroon.

"*Baruch Hashem*," I said. "Why's that?"

"I've started to realize that the reason I can't find answers to the questions that bug me—about the meaning of life, about love and such and such—is not because the answers are not there, but because the questions aren't. 'What is the meaning of life?' is not a question that objectively exists. Same goes for love, same goes for women."

"You mean, instead of thinking in big ways about things, it's better to think in small ways?" I asked. "What you want for now, instead of what you want to be forever."

"That was exactly the problem," he said. "What do you call this—'*thing* of wisdom'?"

"Pearl?"

He sighed. "Yes."

One nice thing about living a life in deferment is that you can worry less about the day-to-day. There aren't big decisions to make so much as slight course-corrections to ensure you're still heading the same way you've always been heading: to heaven or Manhattan or wherever it is you live in your dreams. But once you get this thing of wisdom, everything becomes more complicated. You have to stop living as the person you want to be and start living as the person you are. You fuck with God. You declare your freedom. It feels great, but it can also knock you out.

"There's a Jewish custom that when you build a house, you leave a wall unfinished, as a reminder of the second temple," he said. "So wherever you live, there's always going to be one part that's still raw."

"Cheapskates," I joked.

Cosmo ignored me.

"It's interesting how on the one hand, I'm such a child, and on the other hand, I philosophize a lot," he said.

"I'm like that too," I said. "Parts of me are young, parts are old. I think everyone's like that."

"We're fucked," he said.

We paused under a streetlamp.

"We're not fucked," I said. "We're fine."

Epilogue

Afew weeks after I moved into Crown Heights, Cosmo said something hilarious. Cosmo often said hilarious things, and I often told him as much. I don't remember what he said in this instance, but I do remember telling him he was the funniest person I'd ever met and that I found myself wanting to write down everything he said so I could repeat it later to friends. "You should put it in a book," he said. So I did.

"The impulse to write things down is a peculiarly compulsive one, inexplicable to those who do not share it, useful only accidentally, only secondarily, in the way that any compulsion tries to justify itself," wrote Joan Didion in the essay "On Keeping a Notebook." I share this compulsion and always have. I write down what people say all the time, and since—although he is funnier—he is ultimately no different from anyone else, I wrote down what Cosmo said too, from the moment

I met him. "Not everything I say is funny," he said once, and I wrote that down too. We talked about the fact of the book periodically: Before I sold it, after I sold it, while I was writing. He advised me to include certain information, like the passage from *The Amazing Adventures of Kavalier & Clay*, and he made a suggestion, which I rejected, for the last line: "It should say: 'If you ever want to date Cosmo, you totally should. Drop me a line, and I'll give you his number.'" To that end, and in the spirit of doing some good in this world, if any readers of this book would like to go on a date with my former roommate, you can reach me at rebecca.dana@gmail.com.

As of this writing, Cosmo and Vera are not an item. He is single, and after many months of being *frei*—of devotion only to jujitsu and considerably more experience in the secular world—he is also a new man. He wears contact lenses now. His clothes are modern and cool. He's in outrageously good shape. He joined an online dating site. The last time we met for a drink, which was a few weeks ago, at a bar in the West Village, our very attractive female bartender tried to pick him up. Cosmo shrugs these things off. His life has changed entirely in the two years since we met. He has his motorcycle license now. He's left Fast Trak and got a job at a company in Brooklyn that ships porn, pens and other supplies to truck stops and convenience stations around the country. He is still practicing jujitsu and hoping to become a teacher, like Professor Grey, someday. He has reconstituted Denim Fajita, and they now practice in a studio space across the street from Penn Station, meaning every week he passes through the sidewalk grate steam and the nut vendor cart fumes that still smell to me like the first day in New York. I'm jealous of this and tell him so, but his bandmates won't let him invite me to rehearsal. He has moved out of our old apartment at 621 Crown Street into a one-bedroom outside the Hasidic neighborhood. He is still close with the Goldfarbs and many of his old friends in Crown Heights, but as of this writing, he does not self-identify as a Jew.

Whereas I do—as a Jew, as a New Yorker, as a girl from Pittsburgh, as a journalist and as about a hundred other things. On the outside, I am the same as I've always been. I look the same, except I'm a bit older and my hair is brown now. I have the same job. The only real change is that instead of being alone in the world, I see myself as one of all these people, part of a sprawling community of meaning that stretches from the Goldfarbs' living room to Upper East Side brownstones to the back porch of an old vintage shop in New Orleans. New York has worked its movie magic on me after all. The fairy tale is real. I am in love. I am happy. At the date of the publication of this book, I will be thirty years old.

Acknowledgments

I am grateful first to Cosmo, for letting me invade his life and for giving me a home when I was alone in the world. I am grateful to my editor, Amy Einhorn, for helping to turn this tangled mess of human life into an actual book, and to my agents, Jason Anthony, Rachel Vogel and Sylvie Rabineau, for seeing potential in the story of a lost, lanky Jewish girl long before she got it together. And I am grateful to the rest of my family: to Tina Brown, Edward Felsenthal, Sam P. Jacobs, Bryan Curtis, Gabé Doppelt, Lucas Wittmann, Jacob Bernstein, Tom Watson, David Jefferson, Ben Crair, Tom Weber, Paula Szuchman, Kara Cutruzzula, and everyone else; to Peter Kaplan, Tom Scocca, Choire Sicha, Michael Barbaro, and Michael Solomon; to Richard Plepler and Sheila Nevins; to Claire Howorth, Laury Frieber, Allegra LaViola, Sara Vilkomerson, Lucy Boyle, Mako Ijima, Sara Bernstein, Maria Zuckerman, Lauren Schuker Blum, Rachel Dodes Wortman, Kristin Victoria Barron, Annie Garment, Suzi Garment, Matthew Horowitz, Amanda and

Greg Clayman, Robert and Jennifer Carlock, Jacob and Randi Brookman-Harris, Reihan Salam, Kate Bleich, Davi Bernstein and all the rest of my wonderful friends; to Statler LLC; to the Goldfarbs and everyone else who took me in in Crown Heights; to Francesca Mercurio, without whom I would be lost; to the Angelos—Judy, John, Jack, Kate, Hilary, and François—who have given me the big, beautiful family of my dreams; to my parents, David and Laurie, whose strength and sacrifices made me the person I am today.

And to Jesse, the man at the symphony, who gave me something too good to write about. This book, my life, my love—they are all for you.

READERS GUIDE TO

Jujitsu Rabbi and the Godless Blonde

DISCUSSION QUESTIONS

1. Rebecca has always dreamed of moving to New York and creating a life like Carrie Bradshaw's in *Sex and the City*. When she arrives, she immediately feels like she is home. Why is New York so important to her? What is her perception of the city? Is this perception false? Does it change over time?

2. After first meeting Cosmo and touring the apartment in Crown Heights, Rebecca leaves feeling relieved she'll never see him again. What changes her mind and makes her want to move in? Do you think she sees this as a temporary escape or as a chance to begin a journey of self-discovery?

3. Although they come from completely different worlds, Cosmo and Rebecca become unlikely friends who are each at surprisingly similar crossroads in their lives. Compare and contrast their individual crises—Rebecca as newly single, and Cosmo questioning his faith for the first time. How do they each deal with being thrust outside their comfort zone? Do they sympathize with each other? Why is their friendship so important for each of them during this time?

4. Cosmo's expressions and behavior—such as eating bacon raw—are comedic, although he isn't trying to be funny. Why is he a great character for this book? Would you be his roommate?

5. There is a sharp contrast between the secular world Rebecca lives in in Manhattan—parties, celebrities, fashion, drugs— and her new ultra-Orthodox Brooklyn neighborhood. How is she an outsider in both? In which ways does she belong?

6. Discuss the women Rebecca meets in the Lubavitch community. How are they unlike what she expects? Do you believe they are truly happy? Or are they oppressed, as so many in the secular world believe?

7. After her week at the Yeshivacation, Rebecca realizes she is searching for a "community of meaning." What does this come to mean to her? Does she eventually find it? How?

8. All through her journey, the author is insistent that "We are not in dialogue with the universe." She believes the universe doesn't send signs. Do you think this is true? Was the universe sending her signs? Do you believe in signs, or have examples of when you felt the universe sent you a sign?

9. Has your perception of ultra-Orthodox Jews changed after reading this book? What did you learn about their culture that was unexpected?

10. Rebecca thinks she has achieved her perfect life in the beginning of the book but after her relationship ends, she realizes she still has a lot of work to do. How can a derailment from the life you thought you wanted end up being a good thing? Discuss a time when something threw you off course from the future you thought you would have, and how it turned out.

11. Near the end of her stay in Crown Heights, Rebecca realizes: "You have to stop living as the person you want to be and start living as the person you are." What are the differences between the person she wants to be and the person she is? How does she eventually make peace with her true self?

12. Although surrounded by religion, is this really a spiritual journey for Rebecca? Is her faith or relationship with God altered after living with Cosmo and the Lubavitchers?

13. After returning to Manhattan, has Rebecca changed? What is and isn't different about her? What are the most important things she's learned? How does Cosmo's transformation compare?

About the Author

Rebecca Dana has written for *Newsweek* and the *Daily Beast,* the *Wall Street Journal, Rolling Stone* and the *New York Observer.* She lives in Manhattan with her husband and their dog.